RECLAIMING MY LIFE FROM BROKEN PROMISES

BY CORINNE HOSTENNE

Produced by:

FriesenPress
Suite 300 – 852 Fort Street
Victoria, BC, Canada V8W 1H8

www.friesenpress.com

Distributed to the trade by The Ingram Book Company

TABLE OF CONTENTS

I would like to say a huge thank you to all shelter workers, and social workers in Montréal, Québec and Calgary, Alberta, to my daughter, coworkers and friends for all their love, support, and encouragements.

I would like to thank FriesenPress for all their hard work. To Lisa Fraser, my Author Account Manager; I would like to say a huge "Thank You" for all the time you spent listening to me and answering all of my questions, big or small. Thank you for your patience with me. And to Connie Musto; I feel especially grateful for all the support and encouragement you have given me over the past two years to write this book. Thank you!

I AM SORRY

I am sorry if I made you angry
I am sorry if I did not give you the respect you deserved
I am sorry if I have done anything to hurt
I am sorry for all the times I did not listen to you

I am sorry for all he times I did not do what you wanted me to do
I am sorry for all the times I talked back to you
I am sorry for all the times I said no to you
I am sorry I was not the perfect wife you wanted me to be

I am sorry if I disappointed you
I am sorry if I was not appreciative for all you have done for me
I am sorry if I did not show any appreciation to you
I am sorry if I have done you any wrong

I am sorry that you did not give me a chance to grow and blossom
I am sorry that you did not give me a chance to have my own opinion
and feelings
I am sorry that you did not give me a chance to have my own voice
I am sorry for all the times you hurt me

I am sorry that you made me cry
I am sorry that you did not treat me right
I am sorry that you did not have any respect for me
I am sorry that you hit me

I am sorry that you yelled and swear at me
I am sorry that you cut up my clothing
I am sorry that you choose my clothing
I am sorry that you blame me for your behavior

I HAVE

I have walked away so many times from you
On sure of what life would be like

Fearing the unknown
Fearing of living life alone
Fearing of what is out there
Fearing of facing life alone

So many times I have been back and forth year after year
So many times you lost your temple on me
So many times you get angry with me
So many times I walked away from you

Yet I will always retun
Why I don't know
Why nothing ever change
Yet things still remain the same

Your beatings
Your torments
Your torture
Your hate
Your anger
Nothing, nothing ever gets change

Not for the fact that I would miss you because I would not miss you
But for the simple fact that you told me that I was stupid and that
I cannot do anything for my self
The funny thing was that I believe you

I KEEP TELLING

I keep telling myself that you would change your ways
Change your behavior
You would be much nicer to our daughter and me
You would be a much kinder person

I keep telling myself that you would change your ways
You would stop yelling at me
You would stop cursing at me
You would stop hitting on me

I keep telling myself that you would change your ways
You would stop calling me names
You would stop putting me down
You would stop tormenting me

I keep telling myself that you would change yours ways
You would stop cross-examination me
You would stop judging me
You would stop accusing me of things I didn't do

You would not stop questioning me about what I do when I go outside
When will you stop checking up on me?
When would you stop degrading me in the present of our daughter?
I pray that you would be good to me but you never do

You show no respect for our daughter or for me
I am sick and tired of your accusations
I am sick and tired of you beating up on me
I cannot do anything without your horrible remarks
You are always doing and saying degrading things to me

I cannot do anything without you judging me
Stop judging me
Stop treating me like if I am stupid
You have to stop
Just stop
I am tired
I have no strength left to fight with you anymore
I have No more energy left to defend myself anymore

I feel so alone
You said you love me and that why you treat me the way you do
I don't think that you love me
That's not love
If you love me you will not hurt me like that

THINKING I WAS GOING CRAZY

You make me think
That I was going crazy
You make me think that something was wrong with me
And I really believe you
I really believe something was wrong with me

You were the devil in disguise
You were many people in one
Never knowing who you would be next
You were very scary at times to live with
I was frightened to be with you

Living with you were like living with a crazy person
Never knowing when you would explode
Never knowing when you would lose your temper
You were always mad, mad about everything

You refused to listen to me, or what I had to say
You refused to take advice from me
You tell me you would never take advice from any woman
You asked me why you should take advice from me
"Dam" piece of shit, woman like you
Stupid bitch like me"
Why should you listen to me?

ANGER

Can you see your anger is taking over your life?
Can you see that your anger is taking over our life?
Can you see your anger is hurting your daughter?
Why are you so angry all the time?

This anger you have inside of you will kill you slowly
Can you see this anger is destroying your family?
Can you see this anger is destroying your life?
Your anger is making me sad

Your anger is making our daughter sad
Can you see your anger is destroy the life that we work so hard to build up
Your anger made you do wrong things to your family
Your anger have caused me so much pain, sadness and so much tears

I prayed that you would controlled your anger
I prayed that you would change you behavior
Your anger makes you hate your family
Why do you let your anger take controlled over you?

Your anger destroyed the relationship between you and I
Your anger cause you to lose your family
Your anger cause serious suffering in your family
And In your life

IT TAKES

It takes strength to have hope for the future
It takes strength to say I am sorry to the ones we hurt and love
It takes strength to improve on one self-esteem
It takes strength to improved one self

It takes strength to be truthful to the ones we love
It takes strength to be successful in all we do
It takes strength to feel independent and to have the freedom to controlled
one life
It takes strength to believe in our self

It takes strength to be honest
It takes strength to be forgiving to the one who harm us
It takes strength to accept opportunity and change in one life
It takes strength to be a strong person

It takes strength to deal with difficult choices
It takes strength to have encouragement
It takes strength to be direct with other
It takes strength to be determine

It takes strength to have a positive attitude towards others
It takes strength to take control of our live
It takes strength to take charge of our sef
It takes strength to take charge of our future

It takes strength to be kind to our self
It takes strength to be happy for life and in our lives
It takes strength to encourage another
It takes strength to be thankful

It takes strength to be thoughtful
It takes strength to believe that all things are possible
It takes strength to be self-ass assured
It takes strength to see the beauty in others

It takes strength to give love
It takes strength to make a different
It takes strength to believe in one self

It takes strength to have dreams

It takes strength to be self-assure
It takes strength to be satisfied in all we do
It takes strength to see the beauty in others
It takes strength to love someone others than one self

It takes strength to make a different
It takes strength to believe in oneself
It takes strength to trust
It takes strength to have dreams

It takes strength to keep commitments
It takes strength to be trusting
It takes strength to have a positive attitude
It takes strength to make the impossible possible

It takes strength to feel good of one self
It takes strength to forgive
It takes strength to overcome all struggles and obstacles that comes our way
It takes strength to have patience

It takes strength to have determination
It takes strength to say no
It takes strength to stand firm

GRATEFUL

I am grateful for my daughter who is the apple of my life
I am grateful for God who is the love of my life
I am grateful for Jesus who is the joy of my life
I am grateful for my health that keeps me standing strong

I am grateful for feeling free
For the freeness I feel in Christ Jesus that he give so I can feel as free as a bird in a tree
I am grateful for the freedom, the freedom that I have found in Christ Jesus
I am grateful for the food that I eat that gives me strength
I am grateful for my family, friends, and love ones who make me feel very special

I am grateful for all the good people who stand by me in my time of needs
I am grateful for all the good things in my life and the not so good things in my life
I am grateful for the air that I breath, and most of all I am grateful for life it self
I am grateful for the sunlight, moonlight, daylight, and for the nighttime to

I am grateful for all living things and all breathing things around me
I am grateful for Mother Nature and all her splendor and beauty
Most of all I am very grateful to be alive
And I am grateful for all the love in my life

IT IS TIME

It is time for me to get myself together
It is time for me to get my life together
It is time that I mend my broken heart
It is not as easy as I thought it would be
To put my life back to together
I have to do what is best for me right

I need to heal myself
I need to heal my broken heart
No one will do it for me
I have to stop thinking about the past
And move on with my life

Dwelling on the past will not help me
It just keeps me back
I am the only one keeping myself back, keeping myself down
Stressing myself about the past will not help me
I am the only one holding myself down, holding myself back
I am trying to take it one day at a time

I have to stop stressing myself about the past
What gone is gone?
I have to stop troubling myself about the past
I don't have controlled over the past
But I have controlled over my life and over my thoughts

LIVING WITH

Living with you was too much to take
You made life so unbearable
I was very unhappy

I was very sad
I was very depressed
I had a hard time dealing with everyday life
Because you made life so confusing

Living with was like living in a cage
I have been oppressed
I have been stressed
I have been miserable

I have been disrespected
I have been disregarded
I have been look down upon by you
Living with you was like living in prison

I was trapped between walls that I call my home
I have been swear at
I have been hit
I have been yelled at
I have been cursed at

I was so lost
I have been broken
I was living a life of unhappiness and misery
In the house I call my home

FORGIVENESS

Forgiveness is letting go of the past, and looking toward the future
Forgiveness is letting go of the hurt and healing our hearts
Forgiveness is forgiving friends for causing us pain
Forgiveness is forgiving, love one for the wrong that they has done to us

Forgiveness is letting go of the past and moving on   with our life Forgiveness
is accepting what has happen in our life and dealing with it in a positive way,
Forgiveness is giving our self-time to heal
Forgiving is giving our-self the chance to move forward

Forgiveness is to be able to let go of the old feelings and replacing it with new
and positive feelings,
Forgiveness means that we are starting all over a new
Forgiveness means that we would be all right because we are strong

Forgiveness is the one thing we can do to be whole again and for our self to
begin the process to heal our hearts, mind, body, spirit and soul
Only when we forgive the people who hurt us only then and then we can began
to heal our hearts and our self,

I can now forgive myself and let go of the past and the pain
Forgiveness means to let go of the hurt that was done in our life and look
forward to the future,
Only when we forgive family and love ones
Only then we can completely move on with our life

DETERMINATION

I am determining to survive
I am determining live
I am determining to march forward
I am determining to fight for what I believe in and what I believe is right

I am determining to pick up the pieces and move forward
I am determining to make something out of my life, and my self
I am determining to reach for the sky, and for my dreams
I am determine to never have regrets

I am determining to succeeded
I am determining to take chances
I am determining to make changes in my life
I am determining to reach for the stars

I am determining never to let anyone or anything stand in my way
Or to tell me I cannot do this or do that,
I am determining to not give in or give up
I am determining to reach for my dreams
I am determining never to give up hope in what I believe in

I am determining to always be positive
I am determining to always make my self-happy
I am determining to fight for what I believe in and for what is rightfully mine
Most of all I am determining to live

I FORGIVE MYSELF

I forgive myself for putting myself down
I forgive myself for not believing in myself
I forgive myself for being hard on myself
I forgive myself for yelling at myself
I forgive myself for hurting myself
I forgive myself for thinking that I was ugly
I forgive myself for questioning who I am
I forgive myself for making myself sick
I forgive myself for being angry with myself
I forgive myself for not loving myself
I forgive myself for telling myself that I was stupid
I forgive myself for not trusting myself
I forgive myself for not taking care of myself
I forgive myself for not seeing the beauty within myself
I forgive myself for being negative about myself
I forgive myself for not taking the time to get to know myself
I forgive myself for not wanting to live
I forgive myself for feeling useless
I forgive myself for not seeing the good in myself
I forgive myself for not appreciating myself
I forgive myself for judging myself
I forgive myself for not taking myself seriously

YOU KNOW

You know all the right things to say to make me feel all right
You know how to make everything good in my life
You know how to lift me up when I am feeling down
You have always treated me with respect, as a friend and as a daughter

You have always treated me wonderful
You have always been good to me
You pick my spirit up when it was down
You were sensitive to my wishes and my feelings

You listen to me better than anyone that I know
You understand me so much
You understand how I really feel
You know when I am glad sad or angry

You are a sign that everything is going to be all right
If it was not for your understanding and love, I would not be as strong as I
am today

To my Daughter

CHERISH

The touch of your hands I will cherish forever
The warmth of your smile I will cherish forever

The happiness you have brought into my life I will cherish forever
The happiness you have brought into my heart I will cherish forever

We will always be close to each other no matter the distance
I want to let you know that you are my -everything

And that you mean everything to me
You are my special someone, and my special friend

Sometimes I wonder do you really know how much you meant to me
Well my dear you mean the world to me

And you are my world
Life is beautiful because you cared

You are incredibly special to me
You have brought so much joy into my life and into my heart that would last

A life time oh how wonderful you are to me
You have given me so much encouragement and strength to carry on

I want to tell you that you are beautiful and wonderful to me and that you are
truly special to me

I will cherish every moment we have shared together
You have brought me memories that would last me a lifetime

You keep me standing strong

To my daughter

WHO AM I TO YOU?

You call me your wife
But Am I really, your wife
You had no respect for me what so ever
You treat me more like a stranger than a wife

Who am I to you?
You said that I am your wife
And that I have to take care of you because I am your wife
You need to think that over you also have to take care of me

Because I am your wife
This is a two-way street mister
Stop treating me like maid and start being my husband
Treat me like a husband should treat his wife

I maybe your wife
But I am not your slave that you can treat how you want, and whenever you want
I had no thought of my own, not being able to do anything for myself, not being
able to do on my own.
I maybe your wife
But I am not your toy
That you can play with, tossed around, and dragged rounder when you feel like it

I maybe your wife
But I am not your puppet that you can mimic into doing whatever you want
Think about that
Nothing last for long, nothing last for ever

You can only make me do things your way for a while
I would not be putting up with it for very much longer
I maybe your wife but not for very long
You have no respect for me what so ever

You have no respect for our daughter
You put me down in the present of our daughter
You say nasty degrading things to me in the present of our daughter
You have no respect for your self
You had no idea how to love anyone but you're self

YOU GIVE ME

You give me hope to look forward to each day
You give me courage to believe in my self
You give me strength to carry on
You give me respect, respect I deserved

You give me love that feels my heart to the top
You give me courage to push onward
You give me so much comfort that sooth my broken heart
You give me good thoughts

You give me hope to dream
You give me such joy and happiness
You bring me laughter that keeps me going
You bring me such peace of mind

You give me faith to withstand the pull and tug of life
You give me energy to continue on with my day
You bring me good thoughts to be positive
You give me a positive outlook on life

You make me feel that I can do anything
You give me hope for change
You give me hope to reach my goals and dreams
Most of all you make me believe in myself

WHY THE NEED

Why the need to put me down
Why the need to insult me
Why the need to embarrassed
Why the need to make me feel uncomfortable

Why the need to make me unhappy
Why the need to hurt me
Why the need to tell me how to dress
Why the need for your dirty looks

Why the need to call me ugly
Why the need to call me fat
Why the need to call me stupid
Why the need to call me handicap

Why the need to call me an asshole
Why the need to call me whore
Why the need to call me bitch
Why the need to threatened me

Why the need to destroy my belonging
Why the need to cut up my clothing
Why the need to put my things in the garbage
Why the need to lock me out

Why the need to call me dame piece of shit
Why the need to ignore me
Why the need to tell me that no one will love me
Why the need to humiliate me

Why the need to tell me that I could not do anything right
Why the need to threatened to killed me
Why the need to tell me I was being unfaithful
Why the need to take thing away from me

Why the need to criticized me
Why the need to insult my family and friends
Why the need to turning off the television

Why the need turning off the radio

Why the need to take the house keys away from me
Why the need to throw my dinner in the garbage
Why the need to threatened to take my daughter away from me
Why the need to stop me from working

Why the need for taking my money
Why the need for telling me if I touch the food in the house there would be
blood in this house
Why the need to tell me that our daughter in not your child
You ripped my heart right out of my chest
I have loved you and pay the price for your love
I have felt the pain and the weight of your love

FOR THE WOMEN

For the women who put their lives on the line for us

For the woman who put their security at risk for us

For the women go out of their way for us

For the woman who go the extra mile for us

For the women who tell us that we are beautiful

For the women who tell us we are smart people

For the woman who give us so much

For the woman whose hearts are bigger than the world

For the woman you are all wonderful and beautiful

For the woman who taught us how to love ourselves

For the woman who taught us how we should be treated

For the woman who told us that we are deserved

For the women with the biggest hearts

For the women with the greatest hearts

For the woman who care about us

For the woman who helped us heal our broken hearts

For the woman who taught us what true happiness is?

For the woman who cure what no doctor could cure

For the woman who surrounded us with their love and friendship

For the women who give us the best moments and memories of our lives

For the woman whom we love with all our hearts and souls

For the woman we would like to say thank you very much

For the woman who we love

For the woman who have become our family

For the woman we can put our trust in

For the woman who support us

For the woman who encourage us

For the women who give more than family gives

For the woman who open their hearts and lives to us

THANK

Thank you for being there for me
Thank you for listening to me
Thank you for your encouragement
Thank you for your kind words

Thank you for not judging me
Thank you for caring
Thank you for your patience
Thank you for the time you have spent listening to me

Thank you for taking the time to show that you care
You mean so much to me
You make life much better
For my daughter and myself

You make my light shine through
You put a smile on my face
You make me feel so wonderful
Life is so much better because you cared

I am at peace because you cared
I am grateful because you cared
Life is so beautiful because you cared
I am thankful because you cared

My heart and my soul are at peace because you were there
You lift me up when I was down
You are all my angels
I thank God above that there are people

Like you to help people like me,
I thank God for giving you all the understanding
To understand our feelings and problems
I asked God to bless each and every one of you all

And to keep you all safe in his care
I am proud to have met you
I thank the lord for you all
Because you give so much

I am very thankful to you
Thank you for your support

FRIENDSHIP

A friend is someone who will touch your heart
A friend is someone who will inspire you
A friend is someone sends straight from God
A friend will always hold you dearly in his or her heart

A friend is someone who will bright up your day
A friend is someone who will always be there
A friend will understand your feelings no matter how big or small
A friend will always be there with open arms

A friend will always make you feel special
A friend will have time to share a smile or a hug with you
A friend will always give you hope
A friend is someone we can turn to in times of needs

A friend will always listen to you
A friend will always be true to you
A friend will never let you down
A friend will never let you give up on your self

A friend will always share your dreams and goals with you
A friend is someone who will make you feel as cute as a button
A friend is like a treasure extraordinary and special
A friend will ease your fears and wipe your tears

A friend is someone who will keep your secrets safely tucked away
A friend will add beauty, happiness, joy, and peace to your life
A friend is like a rose rare and special in every way possible
A friend is like a gift special and wonderful in every way never knowing what to
expect or what's inside the box

A friend will always make you feel beautiful
A friend will show compassion towards you
A friend will always listen to you with a keen ear and without judgments
The meaning of a true friend last a long time

IT TAKES PATIENCE

It takes patience to love another.
It takes patience to be gentle.
It takes patience to be a good mother.
It takes patience to listen to our children.

It takes patience to be firm.
It takes patience to listen to a friend in pain.
It takes patience to feel our own pain.
It takes patience to express our own feelings.

It takes patience to heal our hearts, mind, body, spirit, and soul.
It takes patience to overcome our fears.
It takes patience to deal with tough times.
It takes patience to believe in our self.

It takes patience to control our anger.
It takes patience to listen with full attention.
It takes patience to acknowledge our own feelings.
It takes patience to give our self-time to think.

It takes patience to take care of others.
It takes patience to take responsibilities for our own behavior.
It takes patience to be positive.
It takes patience to accept challenges.

It takes patience to accept others without judgment.
It takes patience to forget the past.
It takes patience to deal with difficult times.
It takes patience to discover who we are.

It takes patience to support another.
It takes patience to have a positive attitude.
It takes patience to never give up.
It takes patience to have love.
It takes patience to be kind.
It takes patience to be understanding.

I HAVE THE COURAGE

I have the courage to change my life.
I have the courage to accept things I cannot change in my life.
I have the courage to stand up tall and proud.
I have the courage to be the best that I can be.

I have the courage to be who I want to be.
I have the courage to speak of only the truth.
I have the courage to do anything I put my mind to.
I have the courage to take control of my life.

I have the courage to live my life to the best of my abilities.
I have the courage to go forward in life.
I have the courage to reach my goals and dreams.
I have the courage to take charge of my life.

I have the courage to go wherever I want to go in my life.
I have the courage to be free.
I have the courage to be myself.
I have the courage to live lovingly and fearless.

I have the courage to take opportunities.
I have the courage to accomplish great things.
I have the courage to forgive.
I have the courage to accept any circumstances that comes my way.

I have the courage to accept great things in my life.
I have the courage to be myself and nothing else.
I have courage to accept the sweetness of life or what life has to offer.
I have the courage to accept the beauty of life.
I have the courage to stand up for my self

I HAVE THE RIGHT

I have the right to make mistakes
I have the right to not be perfect
I have the right to choose for my-self
I have the right to controlled my life

I have the right to be the best that I can be
I have the right to be respected
I have the right to set my own goals
I have the right to say yes or no

I have the right to be angry
I have the right to express my feelings
I have the right to feel good about my self
I have the right to my own opined

I have the right not to be judged
I have the right to change my mind
I have the right to be listen to
I have the right to be taken seriously

I have the right to my own thoughts
I have the right not to be abused
I have the right not to be denied
I have the right to my safely

I have the right to my dignity
I have the right not to be force to do thing I don't want to do
I have the right to say I care
I have the right to say I don't care

I have the right to my own feelings
I have the right to my freedom
I have the right not to be criticize
I have the right to say I am hurting

I have the right to my own dreams
I have the right to be happy
I have the right to the best out of my life
I have the right to everything good in my life

I have the right not to be controlled
I have the right to be mad
I have the right to be sad
I have the right to be glad

I have the right to be myself
I have the right to be loved
I have the right to make my own decisions
I have the right to be free

I have the right not to feel scared by any one
I have the right to speak freely

THANK YOU LORD

I thank you lord for being there today
I thank you lord for being in my life
I thank you lord for protecting me
I thank you lord for giving me life

I thank you lord for the birth of my daughter
I thank you lord for always being with me
I thank you lord for the kind of person I am
I thank you lord for your love

I thank you lord for giving me strength
I thank you for giving me a health body, mind, soul, and spirit
I thank you lord for giving me the courage to get out of Montreal in search of
freedom, and for my peace of mind
I thank you lord for your guidance

I thank you lord for keeping me safe and warm
I thank you lord for the food on my table
I thank you lord for the good things in my life
I thank you lord for my friends and family

I thank you lord for all the beautiful people in my life
I thank you lord for your presence in my life

LORD THANK YOU

Lord thank you for making me so much stronger
Lord thank you for making me so much better
Lord thank you for changing my life
Lord thank you for giving your love to me

Lord thank you for making me feel so wonderful and being so wonderful to me
Lord thank you for giving me hope to dream and to wish
Lord thank you for giving me strength to succeed
Lord thank you for giving me courage to create change in my life

Lord thank you for giving me courage and the confident to change my life and
Having confidence in my self
Lord thank you for giving me hope for change
Lord thank you for giving me courage to love

Lord thank you for giving me courage to survive
Lord thank you for calming the hurricane in my life
Lord thank you for calming my trouble heart
Lord thank you for just being there in my times of needs

Lord thank you, and I appreciate you
Lord thank you for helping me change my life
Lord thank you for not judging me
Lord thank you for loving me

Lord thank you for holding onto me
Lord thank you for comforting me in my times of needs
Lord thank you for forgiving my sins
Lord thank you for soothing my broken heart

Lord thank you for bringing me peace of mind
Lord thank you for bringing me changes in my life
Lord thank you for nourishing my mind, body, sprit, and my soul
Lord thank you for feeding my mind with positive thoughts

PEOPLE

In my life I have meet many wonderful people with big hearts
People who are willing to give and not take
People who are willing to listen and not talked over you
People who are truly caring, and loving
People who understand what we are going through
People who would always be there comes rain or shine
People who would always be there with an encouraging word and would always
have a word of encouragement for us
People we can always count on
People who would always be there with open arms, and open hearts
And a broad shoulder to lean on

BE HAPPY

Be happy for who you are
Be happy with who you are
Be happy for the things you have
Be happy for what you don't have

Be happy for the small things in your life
Be happy for the big things in your life
Be happy when you have
Be happy when you don't have

Be happy for your friend's family and love ones
Be happy for the flowers
Be happy for the fresh air
Be happy for sunlight

Be happy for moonlight
Be happy for the stars
Be happy for the rain
Be happy for the snow

Be happy for the wind
Be happy with what you do
Be happy in what you do
Be happy in for life

Be happy in your life

Be happy in all that you do
Be happy with who you are
Be happy for others
Be happy for your self

Be happy for the world and all its speculate, and its magnificence

YOU WERE

You were a sad person
You were a hash person to deal with
You were always passing judgment
You treat me like an object

You were a very mischievous person
You were a hateful person
You were an evil person
You were a very cruel person

You were a hateful person
You were the devil in disguised
You were a very dangerous person
You were a destructive person

You were not a gentleman
You were a hazardous person
You were a melancholy person
You were a deceitful person

You flipped in and out of personality
You were a disrespectful person
You were an uncivilized person
You were a disturbed person

You were a revengeful person
You were a calculating person
You were a deadly person
You were a heartless person

You were a trouble person
You were an un-thoughtful person
You were like a plague
You were unbearable to live with and to deal with

You were an unpleasant person
You were a selfish person
You were an unstable person
You were your own worst enemy

You were a difficult and hard person to live with
You were always blaming me for your wrongdoing
Your wickedness was unbearable to deal with
I were heart broken by your heartless cruelty

ENGOYING MY LIFE

I know longer do things
Because I have to
I now do things
Because I want to

It is amazing to be alive
And it is great to be myself
Life is what we make of it
And life is wonderful and beautiful

I am now enjoying my life
And living my life to the fullest
I am spread my wings and fly
I am being who I was really meant to be

I am being who I always want to be
I am now doing what I always wanted to do,
I am getting to know myself a whole lot better
I am getting in touch with whom I am

And I am special
I just have to remember that there is no one quite like me
I am unique
There is no one quite like me

I am enjoy my life
Since this life is the only one I have
I am live my life honestly and respectfully
I know longer have to wonder

What might have been or what could have been
Because I have controlled over my life today

FEAR

Living in fear was no fun
Living in fear was no picnic
Having to watch over my shoulder
All the time was nerve racking
It was like living in prison

Walking on egg shell
Walking on broken glass
Just waiting, just waiting,
For your next explosion

Never knowing when you would explosion was really scary
I was always scared, scared to talked
Scared to read to our daughter
Because you would yelled at us

And tell us to shut the fuck up
You guys making too much noise
We were scared to turn the television on
Fearing that you would yell and swear at us

To satisfy yourself you would turn the television and the radio of
We was scared to turn television and the radio on
For the fact that you would turn them of
And yelled at us
Living with you was nerve racking
It was like living in prison
I had no thought of my own
No opinions of my own
Never knowing what to expect from you next was nerve wrecking

You would change from nice and calm
To aggressive and violent in minutes
You would yelled at us so loud
Everyone in our building
Would hear your horrible behavior
And the horrible things you would say to us

You would name each piece of clothing
By name that you have bought for me
You would take things away from me like if I were a little child
When you get angry with me

You would take money away from me, and things that you have bought from me
You would cut up my clothing and put them in the garbage
You would destroy things of mine that meant a great deal to me
And things that I like you would yelled at me so hard

My heart would shake with fear
You paralyzed my body, mind, spirit and soul with fear
You telling me if I ever live you, you will kill me
You were always using death treats on me

Always telling me that you would kill me
You instilled a fear in me that cripple me
Mentally, physically, sexually, and spiritual
Always treating me to take our daughter and send her to your country

Always telling me I would not see my daughter any more
Why did you have to tell me one day I would come home and my daughter
would not be there?
Why the need to treat me this way, why, why
Why the need to hurt me like that

I don't think I deserved that kind of treatment from you
What was the need for such horrendous treatment?
You hurt me a great deal, and you treat me so badly
Especially when you tell me if your mother were here
You would put me in the garbage a longtime ago
And if you had a gun you would shout me

I haven't done you any wrong
I have always been good to you
So why such confusing treatment
Why such horrible treatment

You were a very difficult person to deal with
Explaining things to you was like talking to a two years old child
You were like a small child always complaining and wining
Especially when things did not go your way
You made life unbearable for everyone in the house
For our daughter
For your self

And for my self
You were never happy with anything
I am not so show that you were happy with your self

I was so scared to live my daughter alone with you even for a moment
Everywhere I go I would take my daughter with me because you were so cruel
For years I thought and believe that you would take my daughter away from me
And that you would really killed me if I did not do what you wanted me to do
But now I am taking my life back
I am taking back controlled of my life

I don't want to make you angry
But I know you will
Because I would be living you soon
I cannot do this any more
I cannot live like that any more

I am not coming back to you this time
You don't treat me very good
You have no respect for me
I cannot live in fear any more
I am tired of feeling cripple with fear
I am tired of being a slave to fear
I don't want to feel scared to go to sleep at nighttime any more

I don't want to go to bed and wake up on the bedroom floor any more
You say I make you angry
And that's why you hit me
That's why you treat me the way you do
I am putting a stop to this feeling of fear today
I am putting a stop to this madness in my life
This has to end today

DON'T TRY TO CHANGE ME

Don't try to Change Me into Something I am not
Don't try to change me in to someone I am not
Shy I am
Stupid I am not
Confused I am
Crazy I am not

Don't try to change me
You choose my clothing
You tell me how I should dress myself
I am not a child
Stop treating me like one

You complained about everything I did or didn't do
You were never happy with anything I did
I could not do anything right where you was concerned
I could not do anything to please you
You were so hard to pleased, and so hard to deal with

Nothing I did pleased you
I try my very best
But even my best was not good enough where you were concern
I try the hardest I know how to please you but still my hardest was in vain
My hardest was not my hardest
My best was not my best
I don't know what else to do

I don't know what to do any more
I am so lost
I am confused
Can someone please help me find my way?
Please, please can someone help me?
You made me into something and someone I am not
You turn me into a scared little child
I am to scared, too scared to talk to anyone
Too scared to speak up for my self

Don't try to change me into something I am not
Don't talked down to me, talked to me

Don't talked at me, talked to me
Don't try to change me someone I am not
Don't looked down at me
Looked at me
Don't yelled at me
Talked to me
Don't hit me
Talked to me

Don't try to change me
I am all that I can be and much more
I am all that you see
Everything you see of me is of me

I am the only me there will ever be
Just let me be myself
And I will be the very best that I can be
Don't try to change me
Everything you see of me is of me

I am all that I can be
I am somebody
I am someone
I am me no one will ever do
But me

YOU BROKE MY HEART

You broke my heart
You broke my spirit
You try to killed me a slow death
You hurt me very badly

You took my strength
You accused me of things that I cannot even began to mention
You never stopped wanting and demanding more and more from me
You always wanted more and more and then some more

You killed me on the inside
You killed me a slow death
A slow death on the inside
My death was a death of silence
No one knew but me

I pretended, pretended, far too long
I cannot pretended any more
I am hurting
Hurting so badly
On the inside no one really know but me

No one really cares any way
No one really understands
If anyone listening to my problems
They don't have anything good to say anyway

I feel so alone in this world
I feel so ashamed
I feel so lonely
And so depressed

I endure you're abused, you're degrading name calling, you're put downs,
You're yelling, you're cursing, you're blaming, and you're beatings
What else do you want from me?
What else can you do to me?

ALL YOU

All you did was bring me down
You made me wear a frown all day long, all night long
You turn me into a clown
All you did is put me down
You have made a fool out of me
You were stifling me
Squeezing the life right out of me
You were like a nagging itch that would not go away
Your love was like a sickness
Your jealousy got the best of you and it got you no way
Your controlling behaviors cause you our marriage, family, and our friendship
You were a bad influence for our daughter

LOVE DOES NOT DEMAND

You demanded so much from me
You asked so much from me
You took so much away from me

I did what you told me to do
I did as I was told
You were so demanding
You were always complaining
Never being satisfied

Making life unbearable for everyone in the home
What is a home if there is no love, and no peace?
You were the devil in disguised
You were always angry
Having to deal with your anger was very terrifying
You walking around with chip on your shoulders

Like if you are the only person with problems in the world
Everyone and everything made you angry
You talk about woman like if we are nothing
I feel sorry for you
And I prayer that you would change your ways

I DON'T KNOW

I don't know who I am any more
I am so lost
Lost somewhere inside my self
I have been lost, lost a long, long time ago

I don't know if I can find my way back any more
I am so angry
So dam angry
No one but me know how angry I am feeling

I am a sad and lost person
Who everyone takes for granted
I feel so hollow on the inside
I feel like there is an empty space inside of me

Just waiting to be filled up
I feel so mix-up
I feel as if no one understands me
Feeling so alone

Feeling like something is wrong with me
I feel like if something is missing in my life
What is my problem?
What is wrong with me?

Why do I feel like I am the only person in the world?
I feel very sad and I don't know why
All I want to do is cry all the time
And I don't know why

YOU

You hit me
You yelled at me
You curse at me you call me the most degrading names in the book
You call me stupid bitch, ugly, fat, bitch, whore, handicap, fat cow,

You said I sleep like a cow
You call me garbage
So tell me something
If I am all, those things, you say I am why do you want me back?

Why do you want me in your life?
What do you want with me?
Why can't you live me alone?
Stop harassing me

Stop treating me as if I am stupid
Stop threatening my life
Live me alone
Get out of my life for good
Goodbye

MONSTER

I have a monster in my life no one knows the feelings but me
I am always hiding this monster
Hiding it in my closet
Hiding it in a corner
Hiding it in whatever dark place I can find
Most of all I am hiding it within myself so that no one
Would really know that I am fighting with this monster

MY DEMON

I have a demon
No one
See it but me

It haunts me day and night
I am always running away
From my demon

There is no way for me to hide
From my demon
I am the only one
Who knows that it's there?

My demon never live me alone
No matter what I do
Or where I go it seems to find me
Dealing with this demon is to
Much for me to take

Who can I turn to for help?
Would they think I am stupid?
Can anybody really help me?
Is there anyone who can really help me?
Because this demon is too great for me to handle on my own

It is greater than I had anticipated
I cannot fight it by myself any more
I am fighting a losing battle
A losing battle is what I am fighting

I may have to go away for a while
I hope that my demon don't follow me
I hope that this will be the end of all my trouble all I want is a little peace in
my life
I have to get away from here

EVERYONE

Everyone had problems but you; you blame me and everyone else for your mistakes
Nothing was ever your problem or your mistakes
Nothing was ever your fault
It was always someone else fault
Or someone else problem
When will you start taking responsibility for your actions?
When will you stop blaming me and everyone else for your behavior?
Grow up and take responsibility for your actions
Stop blaming everyone else for your problems

I AM IN

I am in pain
No one
Know but me
The pain
I feel inside
No one know but me

All I can do is cry
I cannot help myself
I am hurting so much
This wound never heals

I am trying to mend my broken heart
But I don't know how
I try to make peace with my fears
I try to make peace with my self
But it is very hard

Someday I will walk away and free myself from you

CRYING

Crying is the only thing
I can do
To make myself feel better
I am in pain and I don't know why
I feel sad all the time
I feel so down all the time
Thank God for my daughter
Who is here to support me?
What would I have done without you my love?

CLOSE MY EYES

I close my eyes
And I try to forget the past, and the pain
I try to forget the bad words you say to me
You hurt me really badly
You almost demolish my mind
You killed me a slow death on the inside
You destroy my happiness
You take a way my joy,
My peace, my freedom
You cause me so much pain, sorrow, sadness, hate, and anger
I have a very hard time trusting

I DON'T REMEMBER

I done remember ever being happy
All I remember was being alone sad and lonely
And angry as a young girl
My feelings I try to hide

My thought I keep to my self
Any way no one really listen to me
I have learned how to hide my feelings very well
I have learned how to pretend to make everyone think that I was ok

I must go on
Life must go on
I have to survive
I must stay strong

I must not let you see
That I am weak
There were times when I wanted to disappear

YOU SAID

You said to me that you would
Make me walked the streets
You would make me sell my body
You would make my daughter have no respect for me
You would make my life a living hell
You would destroyed my life
Well go right are head do what
Ever you think is right
Do what you want I don't really care any more
I have never done you anything wrong
I don't understand
Why would you want to hurt me?
Why would you want to destroy my life?

YOU CALL ME

You call me a no body, you said that I was nothing, a nobody, and nobody
love me
And when you found me on the streets of Montreal you turn me into a lady
You stupid crazy fool what do you meant for your information I was always a
lady and I am always a somebody

You call me whore
You call me a bitch
You said that I stink as a fish
You said that it was you who teach me how to be civilized

What a joke
What a joke you were
You teach me how to be civilized
Harry now you are being funny

Tell me something boy who teach how to be civilized
For someone who beat his wife
Yelled at his wife
Swear at his wife degrade his wife

Degrade his wife to make her feel like nothing
Name calls his wife in the presence of his child
Throw things because you think it look too good for me
Destroyed things that don't belongs to you

Throw tantrum
Act like a child because you did not get your way
Now tell me Harry who is uncivilized
You beat your wife to make your self-feel like a man

Harry you are the uncivilized one
Take responsibility for your actions
And act like a man
And you tell me no one care about me but you
No one love me but you
Tell me something what kind of love is that?

A GOOD FRIEND

A good friend is one of the rarest to find
A good friend would always look beyond your failures
A good friend would be happy for you when you succeeded
A good friend would hold your hands when you feeling down

A good friend would always put a smile on your face
A good friend would add beauty to your life
A good friend would always be there no matter what
A good friend would always stared you in the right direction

A good friend would always be there when you need a shoulder to cry on
A good friend is someone you can count on
A good friend would make your sky shine like the sun
A good friend would always make you feel good about your self

A good friend would look out for you in difficult times
A good is like music to the heart
A good friend would know your likes and dislikes
A good friend would not let you beat up on your self

A good friend would help you to blossom and flourish
A good friend would always step in, in times of need
A good friend would always stand up for you
A good friend is like plants just water it and watch it grow

A good friend will never let you down
A good friend will never hurt you

I AM IN

No one know
But me
The pain I feel inside
No one; no one but me know how I really feel,
No one know the pain I feel inside
All I can do is just cry
I cannot help myself from crying I am hurting so much
The wound never heals
I try to mend my broken heart
But I don't know how
I try to make peace
With my demons but they stronger than I am
I try to make peace
With myself and with my fear
But it very hard
So I would take it one day at a time

I AM TIRED

I am tired of all the fighting
I close my eyes
And I try to forget the past,
I try to forget the frightening and horrible words you said to me
You hurt me tremendously
You almost destroyed me
You killed me a very slow death on the inside
You take away my happiness
My joy, my peace, and my freedom
All you give to me was sorrow, pain sadness,
And you show me hate and anger

A FRIEND

A friend will support you in your time of need
Friend is like a gift to each other
A friend is someone you turn to in times of trouble
A friend is like a treasure rare and special in every way
A friend is always there with a shoulder when you need one to lean on
We cherish our friends always
Friends will add beauty and joy to your life
A friend is one you can always count on when you need them
A friend will always bright up your life
A friend is like a flower beautiful in every way
A friend will always put a smile on your face
A friend will be happy when you are happy
A friend will always make time for you know matter what
A friend will care about how you feel and respect your feelings
A friend is someone who you can lean on in time of trouble

I NEED TO BE

I need to be free
I need to have my freedom
I need not be limited
I need not be on a chain
I need not be in prison
I don't know who I am anymore
I feel so
Are shamed
So fat
So ugly
So useless
So stupid
So unloved
So alone
So lonely
So tired
So misplaced

YOU WOULD WHAT

You would make me walked the streets of Montreal
You would make me sell my body
You would make my daughter have no respect for me
You would destroyed my life, well go right are head I don't know how much
more can you Hurt me any more do whatever you want, do whatever you think
is right I really don't care anymore what You do to me
Killed me, hurt me go right ahead make your voodoo
Make me walked the streets I really don't care
I have never done you anything wrong
So I don't know why you would want to hurt me in that way
You mean you really hate me that much
To make voodoo on me you would really make me walked the streets of Montreal
I don't understand why you would want to hurt me like that
You said you would destroyed my life and you really meant that
Why do you want to hurt me so much?
And why do you hate me so much
If you don't love me any more you don't have to hurt me that way

CALL ME NOTHING

Call me nothing and telling me that know body love and want me
Telling me that I was no body and nothing
Why did you have to play with my mind like that?
Stop telling me you found me on the street?

And that you made me in to a lady
You crazy fool what a joke you are
If you haven't notice I was a lady when you meet me
And I was somebody when you meet me

You call me uncivilized
Tell me something who is the uncivilized one
And you calling me a whore and a bitch
You said that I stink as a fish

You said it was you that teach me how to be civilized
Looked around mister take a good look whom are you kidding?
What a joke
What a joke you are you teach me to be what

To be civilize now you are being funny
Who teach who how to be civilize
For someone who beat up on his wife
Yelled at his wife

Call his wife degrading names
Throw things
Destroyed things that don't belongs to them
Act like a child

Tell me something who is un- civilized
You say nobody love me but you
No bodies care for me but you
What kind of love is this?

You hit your wife to make yourself feel like a man
You are the un-civilized one
Take responsibility for you actions
And act like a man

And by the way you say you love me
If this is love I don't want to know what hate is

NO ONE

No one deserved to be abused
In any way shape or form
Hurting someone is not the way to get attention
It is not the way to have your voice heard

Hurting someone is no love
Raising your hands towards your wife girlfriend and your children is not love
Slapping your wife of girlfriend would not make you look big
Believe me you look stupid and you would lose your wife or girlfriend

Hurting someone does no one any good
If you don't love someone let them go on their merry own way
Just don't hurt them
Telling someone you love them truing around and hurting them don't make any
sense to me at all

How can you say you love someone and willfully hurt him or her?
Why, why, tell me why
Just let each other go their own way

A MOTHER'S

A mother's love never fails
A mother has a special touch and she is special
She always knows just the right things to do and say
To make her children feel good
She love her children unconditional and would do anything for them
mothers are patience, special, understanding, compassionate, and loving
a mother will always be there with an open arms
And will always be there with a hug
And a kiss to make everything all better
She will always have a smile too bright up ones day
She is loving and caring
she always makes everyone feel happy
when we gets our hearts broken she is always there with a kind word and a
shoulder to lean on
She takes the time to listen
And she tries to fix things the best way she knows how
And always they're with a special touch and a kind word
She is warm, sweet and gentle
She is wonderful to have around
A mother is special in every way
She always knows what best for her children and family
you'll always be in my heart mom
I love you

I AM NOT

I am not perfect
I am not an angel
But I did not deserved
To be treated like that
You had no right
To putting your hands on me like that,
You had no right making me feel less than whom I am
I need to get away from you
I need to get away from here
I need some peace
I deserved better than you
Only a coward hit his wife
Used death treats on his wife
Use forceful violence
What kind of man were you

HOME

Home should be the place where we should feel safe
For some people home is not always a safe place
For some people home is a battlefield
Fighting to stay alive

Fighting to survive
Every day is a struggle
Home is not always a peaceful place
Home is not always the place most people want to be

In most homes there are abuse going on
There are secret crimes going on that are not visible to the human eye
Our homes should be a place where we should feel comfortable safe and free
A home is a place where we should have friendship, compassion, trust, honesty,
happiness, joy, peace,

warmth, laughter, hugs, kisses, unconditional, love,
Thoughtfulness, gentleness, kindness, respect, caring, loyalty, humour, friendli-
ness, unfortunately, for some people home is anything but safe it is more like a
war zone
That's is not a home, this is not the place most people want to be
A home without love is not a home

THANK YOU

Thank you for being there for me
Thank you for encouraging me
Thank you for your kind words
Thank you for not judging me

Thank you for caring
Thank you for your patience
Thank you for the time you spend listening to me
Thank you for making life much better
For my daughter and myself

You make my light shine through
You put a smile on my face
You make me feel so wonderful
Life is so much better because you cared

Life is beautiful because you cared
Life is so, so, beautiful because you cared
I am thankful because you cared
I am grateful because you cared

I am at peace today because you cared
I am free today because you were there
I am myself again because you were there
My heart and soul are at peace because you were there

You lifted me up when I was down
You are all my angels
I thank God above that there are people
Like you to help people like me

I thank God for giving you the understand
To understand our feelings and problems
I asked you lord to bless each and every one of you all

And to keep you safe in his care

I am proud to meet you all
I thank the lord for you because you give so much

I am very thankful to you all
Thank you all for your support

THIS IS MY LIFE

This is my life and I am taking controlled of my life
I am taking the power back from you
I have the power to controlled my own life
I have the power to controlled my destiny
I have the power to take controlled of my well-being
No one can take controlled over my life but me
I am the one person who holds the keys to my life
I am the one in controlled
Not you no more

I JUST

I just want to lie down just for a while
I just want lie down to die
I just want to close my eyes and never open them again
I just want to say good-bye to this sad life
I just want to say good-bye to this sadness I feel in side
I just want to say good-bye to this emptiness I feel in side
I just want to say good-bye to the hole I feel in my heart
I just want to say good-bye to all the bad things that ever happen in my life
I want to say good-bye to this sadness I feel in my heart
The pain I feel in my heart is too great for me to handle
But I know longer want to suffer this pain
I just want to lie down just for a while

I FEEL

I feel like if I am being
Pulled in so many different directions
It is a dark and lonely road to travel
You took what was not yours

And destroyed it
Why did you have to do that?
Why did you hate me so much?
What have I done that was so wrong to you

I feel trapped
You put me through so much pain and sorrow
I have lost my way so many times
I don't know how to find my way back

I am a prisoner in my own home
Not being able to talked to my friends
Not being able to choose my own clothing by my self
Not being able to go out side

And come back home without being interrogate
And made to feel like if I had just commit a crime
You desperately try to demolish my mind, body, spirit, and soul
You have confused my mind

You have put damp on my spirit
You cause confusion in my head
What more do you want from me
What more can you do to me

I don't have anything more for you to take
You have already took everything
There is nothing left for you to take any more

I REFUSED

I refused to dwelled on my mistake's
I refused to dwelled on my disappointment's
I refused to dwelled on what might have been
I refused to be unhappy any more
I refused to take care of everyone except my self
I refused to be controlled by anyone any more
I refused to dwelled on the past
I refused to stress myself over you
I refused to drive my self-crazy
I refused to stay with you
I refused your forceful behavior
I refused to be torment by you any more

CALGARY

I am now beginning to understand myself
Being here has helped me to forget
The terrible things that happen in my life over the years
I am at peace with myself now
I am not in as much pain as I once were

Being here has done wonders for me
I am now at peace with myself, peace with who I am
I can breathe with ease
I no longer have to look over my shoulders

I no longer fear to walk the street
I don't have to worry myself about who is standing next to me any more
No one would understand what I am talking about if you never been in my situation,
Today I can walk with ease, walked without fear

I can take deep breaths and relax
Do you know what that feel like?
That's the feeling of freedom
The feeling of freeness

Calgary represents independence to me
Calgary is the place where I truly find myself
Where I truly find who I am
Moving out here was the best thing I have ever done for myself
And for my daughter

I have learn to let go and to forgive
I have found stillness within my heart, and within myself
I have found enjoyment
I have found myself here
And most of all I have found true happiness and peace

MY HUSBAND

You were my husband
So I thought
I was taught
To obey my husband
And so I did,

So I thought if my husband wanted
To have sex and I did not
It was his right to have sex with me any way
And so you did because that was your right so you say

But if that is true then
Why did I feel dirty?
Why did I feel so sick?
Why did I crying?

Why did I feel this way?
Why did you have to force you're self on me
I said no to you, you said that I am your wife

And that was your right
And so it was
It was your right

YOU DAMAGE MY

Heart
My soul
My body
My self-esteem
You turn me into something and someone I am not
You turned me into a liar
And a sneaky person
You cause me so much pain
So much mistrust
I had to sneak around if I wanted to talked to my friends or anyone else

MY LOVE

I don't think you know how much you really meant to me
You have touched my heart in a very special way
When you embrace me with your soft and gentle hands
You filled my life with your sweet love
My world become your world
Your world become my world
To my daughter

YOU ARE MY STRENGTH

You are my strength
Your present is most appreciated in my life
You help me in my times of my needs
You held my hand in times of trouble

You are an important part in my life
You are the part that brings out the best in me and in my life
How can I not love you?
You will be in my heart forever

You will be in my thoughts always
Every time I think of you it makes me happy
I feel all-tingling on the inside
You have changed my life in so many ways

You brought everything good in my life
Because of you I have so much courage in my self
And so much love for my self
Because of you I have so much strength in myself

Because of you I am the person I am today
You make me so happy
You are so important to me
You bring out the best in me

You have brought me such inner peace
You are so special to me
You are a blessing to me
You are just what I needed in my life

You complete me with your love

To my friend

THANK YOU

Just to say I appreciate you being in my life

Sometimes people come into our lives they leaves such an in print on our lives that would make us think that life is wonderful, sweet, and worth living for sometimes those people stay in our live, and sometime they just pass through and sometimes we don't get the chance to say to those people thank you, and to let them know how much they really meant to us and that we appreciate and love them,

For helping change our life or thank you for helping us to see things clearly in our life and thank you for helping us to see how beautiful and special we are Just to say thank you

YOU KNOW

You know all the right things to say to me
You know how to make things better
You lift me up when I was down
You have treated me with respect
You have treated me good
You have been good to me
You pick my spirit up when it was down
You was sensitive to my needs, and my feelings
You listen to me better than anyone that I know
You understand so much about me
You understand how I feel
You know when I was glad, sad, or mad
You are a sign that everything is going to be all right
If it was not for your understanding I would not be as happy as I am today

YOU GIVE ME

You give me hope to look forward to each day
You give me encouragement to believe in my self
You give me strength to carry on
You give me respect, respect I deserved

You give me love that feels my heart to the top
You give me courage to push onward
You give me so much comfort that sooth my heart
You give me good thoughts

You give me hope to dreams
You give me such joy and happiness
You bring me laughter that keeps me going
You bring me such peace of mind

You give me faith to withstand pull and tug of life
You give me energy to continue on with my day
You bring me good thoughts to be positive
You give me a positive outlook on life

You make me feel that I can do anything
You give me hope for change
You give me hope to reach my goals
Most of all you make me believe in my self

For my dear friends who shown me true love

I MEET A WOMAN

I meet a woman beautiful is her name
She moves with such grace
She is beautiful to look at, sweet to the scent
Gentle to the touch and soft to hold onto

She is nice to talked to
She is everything you need in a friend
She is the mother I have always dreamed of having
She is the sister I have always wanted in my life

She is everything I need in a friend and much, much more
She listens to me attentively and her reply makes you think
Her advice is always true and clear
Her love is real pure and true

HER HEART IS PURE AND
SHE GIVES FREELY TO

Friend's family and love ones
She is a loving and caring person
And she makes my world a whole lot brighter and better

She is like the stars that that shine so bright in my life
She bring out the best in me
She is warm gentle and sweet

THANK YOU

Thank you for being there for me
Thank you for listening to me
Thank you for your encouragement
Thank you for your kind words

Thank you for not judging me
Thank you for caring
Thank you for your patience
Thank you for the time you have spent listening to me

Thank you for taking the time to show that you care
You mean so much to me
You make life much better
For my daughter and myself

You make my light shine through
You put a smile on my face
You make me feel so wonderful
Life is so much better because you cared

I am at peace because you cared
I am grateful because you cared
Life is so beautiful because you cared
I am thankful because you cared

My heart and my soul are at peace because you were there
You lift me up when I was down
You are all my angels
I thank God above that there are people

Like you to help people like me,
I thank God for giving you all the understanding
To understand our feelings and problems
I asked that God to bless each and every one of you all

And to keep you all safe in his care
I am proud to have met you
I thank the lord for you
Because you give so much

I am very thankful to you
Thank you for your support

YOU HAD NO RIGHT

You had no right
To abused me
You had no right
To hurt me

You had no right
To confused my mind
You had no right
To hit me

You had no right
To put me down
You had no right
To play with my emotion

You had no right to
Cause me so much pain
You had no right
To cause such fear in me

You had no right
To falsely accused me
You had no right
To verbally attack me

You had no right
To caused me so much heart ache
You had no right
You had no right to force yourself on me

You had no right to destroy my things
To make me cry

ALL

All you did is bring me down
You made me wear a frown all day long, all night long
You turn me into a silly clown
All you did is put me down
You have made a fool out of me
You were stifling me
You were like a nagging itch that would not go away
Your love was like a sickness
You were a bad influence for our daughter

YOU DESPERATELY

You desperately try to destroy my mind, body, spirit, and soul
You have confused my mind
You have put a damp on my spirit
You cause confusion in my mind
You have made me think that I was going crazy
You made me think that something was wrong with me

LIFE

Life would be much better if we concentrate on the good things in life
Than always on the bad things
In life things will always go wrong
We have to spend more time being positive
And less time being negative
Negativity will hold us imprisoned
And it keeps us from moving forward

I FEEL

Like if I am being
Pulled in many different directions
And it's a dark and lonely road to travel
You took what was not yours
And destroyed it
I feel trapped
You put me through
So much pain
So much sorrow

SOME PEOPLE SAY

That love is blind
For me I don't know if love is blind
But I know for some people
Love can be blind, dangerous, and deadly

And I mean really deadly
We take an oat
When we get married
And it goes something
Like this

I promise to love you in sickness and in health
For richer and poorer
I promise to love you till death do we part

And you took your
Vow very seriously
Specially the part that say
Till death do we part?

YOU USED

You used tricks
You used violence
You used force
You played with my emotions

You used blackmail to get your way
You used fear to controlled me
You used manipulation to keep me in check
You said to me

If I love you
I would what do whatever you want
And you call me selfish
Because I did not give you controlled over my body one night

You got so mad
You lost your temper so badly on me
You cursed at me
You yelled at me

You hit on me
You asked me to get out from your bed and from your room
Before you used your feet to kick me out of your room
I silently got out of your bed

And out of your room
Because I did not want you to
Kicked me out

All this was because I did not want to have sex with you
You forget one thing
This is my body
You have no controlled over it any more

You cannot do what you want with my body and with me any more
I have rights
No means no if I don't want to have sex with you
I have the right to say no
And you have no right to force yourself on me

Even if I were your wife
No still means no
My body is my temple

You have to respect for my body
You have no right to force yourself on me
I need to free my self of this fear I am feeling

I need to let go
You hold me back
For far too long
You keep me down for far too long

I need to be set free
I need to get away from here
I need to get away from you

THERE COMES

There comes a time in ones life
When enough is enough?
I have to stop and think about what I really want
In my life or out of life

I reach that point in my life
Where I have enough
I am taking my life back
I am taking back controlled of my life

I am taking controlled of my destiny
And of my thoughts
I have thoughts of my own
I will not allowed you or anyone to treat me like a fool any more
I will not allowed anyone to treat me like a little child any more

I am tired of this
I am tired of feeling this way
I am tired of this kind of life
I am tired of the controlled

YOUR HANDS

Your hands around my neck
My hands holding on to yours
I try to scream but not a sound came out
I am gasping for air
You began shaking me
Holding me down on the kitchen floor
Slamming my head back and forth on the kitchen floor
Dragging and pulling me around the kitchen
Kicking and screaming that's all I can do
But you don't care
You continue like if it was
The right thing to do
You were hurting me you drag me around the kitchen
Like if I was a mop or a broom

YOU DON'T UNDERSTAND

You don't understand what I am going through
Don't judge me
If you never experience domestic violence
You will not understand
What women like me go through?

Or what it's like for me
If you don't understand what I am going through
Don't pass judgments on me
If you don't understand domestic abuse
Don't say things that you don't know

Please don't say negative things about what you don't understand
I heard you saying woman who
Stay with the men who abused them
Is because they like it that's why they stay
And those women are stupid

Let me tell you something my friend I am not stupid
And so are the billions of other woman who are being abused
Right now by the men who they love an the men who claim to love them
Women like us are not stupid

We only want the same things you want
Which is happiness and to keep our family together
And sometimes we would do that at any cost

Even if that means staying in an abusive relationship
We are not stupid
We just want to keep our family together

GOOD-BYE AND WELCOME

Good-bye my tears
Welcome happiness

Good-bye my sadness
Welcome joy

Good-bye my loneness
Welcome friendship

Good -bye my pain
Welcome delightfulness

Good-bye fear
Welcome freedom

Good-bye depression
Welcome peace

Good-bye difficulty
Welcome tranquility

THE BIRTH OF MY DAUGHTER

I can't believe that I had a hand in creating such a wonderful bundle of joy a
perfect little angel you are,
You change my life
My life will never be the same no more
you filled my life with wonders and hope
you are my bundle of enjoyment
You are my little miracle that came true
Precious and sweet
And adorable to me
You are my little bundle of joy
Unique and special you are to me
Awesome and beautiful you are to me
You have brought so much joy to me
You are my bundle of joy to have around
You are the one who keep me going

I AM ALL- ALONE

Empty and lost
what can I do
where I can go?
What would people say?

Who would believe me?
Everyone think my husband is a nice person
They don't see him the way I see him
They don't know him the way I know him

He let people see what he want them to see
He seems to have respect for other people but not for me
What have I done wrong?
Where did I go wrong?

Life is not what I thought it would be
Nothing is right
I don't seems to do anything right
I need to talk to someone

But whom can I talk to?
Who can I trust?
Who can I turn to?
I have to be careful to who I talk to

Or what can I say to any one
And what I say to anyone
If he fined out that I talk to anyone he will surely kill me
I want to see my daughter grow up

I really don't want to die stupid
I want to see her off to school
I want to see my daughter graduate high school, college, and university
Emptiness is what I feel inside this minute

No one will really understand how I really feel
No one really know what I am going through
They all think he is nice
But really he is not

It is not my place to tell them that
They would find out one day by them self

PEACEFULNESS

I imagine my self
In a peaceful place
Just me myself and I
No one else

Just walking through
A beautiful garden
Beautiful in every way
With wonderful sweet smelling flowers

Of all kind
Of all sizes
Of all shapes
Of all colors

Oh so wonderful
The smell oh so beautiful, wonderful, and sweet,
The colors are so amazing
It's a place where I can find myself and be myself
It a place where I can find peace, happiness, and joy

It's a place where I can relax and be one with nature and with my self

I ASKED MYSELF

I ask myself why did I stayed with him
I tell myself it was easier to stay
Because if I live him I would lost my daughter
Or my life,
He told me if I ever live him he would find the best lawyer there is

And take my daughter
Away from me
He would send her to his country
And I would never see my daughter anymore
I believe him

I am staying for my daughter sake
I am only staying because of
My Daughter she needs her mom
And I need my daughter
everyone call me stupid for staying
with him they say I asked for it
And whatever he does to me I deserve it
No I did not deserve that kind of terrible treatment he made a choice
To treat me unkind

He made the choice to hurt me
Any way if you were in my position
You would do the same thing
For your child or children
You would stay just the same

Stop judging me
You are not in my place
You don't understand
Because I love my daughter
And I am staying for her sake

THEY ALL LOOKED AWAY

And pretend not to see or hear anything
And not to understand
What I am going through,
There left me alone with my struggles, and confusions
they turned their eyes and they heads the other way
pretending not to see anything
Pretending not to hear anything,
But there all stare in silence they all are whispering and gossiping
About things they don't understand
They say that I am stupid to stay with him
And I like the way he treat me that's why
I stay with him
Why do you talk about me behind my back when you don't even understand?
What I am going through
when you don't understand what I am going through
Stop your silly staring and empty chattering

I TOLD MYSELF

I told myself just be strong
but I was not strong enough
I have learned to please
but I have not please enough
I did my best
but my best was not my best
I gave it my all
but my all was not my all
I try to be strong
But I was not strong enough
I try to please
But did not please enough
I try my best
But my best was not my best
I give it my all
But my all was not my all
I have learn it is very hard to please some people

WENT BY

Time went by but
Nothing changes in our home, or in our lives, in our relationship, in our marriage
I have learned to adjust myself to suit you ways
I have learned to not make him angry or mad
I knew my place in the home
I knew my place in the relationship for the most part I learned to stayed quiet
You was most happy when you was the only one doing the entire talking, hitting,
yelling, swearing, name-calling, and controlling,
I knew who was boss in our home
And I don't dare say ant thing
Or question him,
I have learned how to please
I have learned how to pretend
Pleasing was my first name, my middle name, and my last name wound you
believe that it's the truth
I have learned just what not to say to him
I have learned to not upset him
I have learned to be quiet
I have learned to prepare meals just the way he likes it
And no other way was good enough for him but his way
He was most happy when he had controlled over me
And everything else in our relationship

TO DAY

Today I have learned to stand up for my self-yes I have
And to set myself free from you and your torments
That you have caused me no more I am not taking this anymore
I would no longer be abused by you any more

Today I open my mouth for the very first time
I speak up for myself today yes I did
I tell you It shock my husband
He was not expecting me to do that

He never let me talk for myself
And he never listens to me before
He said he don't take advice from any woman
But today I did you should of seeing his face
Then he said look at you, look at you, you talking
When I am talking no one asked you to talk he said to me

I did not asked you to talked he said to me
Did I asked you to talked
Coming closer to my face
Grabbed me by my arms and began shaking me
Yelling and screaming at me

Pushing me up against the wall
And I said to him you couldn't do this to me any more
I am a person just like you
I have feelings just like you
Why are you doing this to me?
Who are you?
You are not God gift to woman

He reply what did you say to me
I said you are not God gift to woman
He yelled and swears at me
Call me degrading names

Look at you he says to me, I do everything for you,
Everything I do is for you and you talking to me like that
You have no respect for me,

You have no respect for me

The clothing you are wearing
I buy it is that right tell me stupid,
You are really stupid,
You are really a stupid person do you know that

The food you eat I buy it isn't so
The bed you sleep on I bought it
Look at you, you sleep like are cow
The roof over your head I pay for it right
Look at you

You cannot do anything for yourself
What do you good for?
Tell me useless piece of shit,
Dam piece of shit,

I yelled out at him do you think you are a gift from God to women
Well you are not I yelled out at him
You cannot do this to me any more
I speak up for myself to day

THE PLACE WE CALL HOME

Sometimes the place we call home is no place to call home?
Sometimes our homes is the worst place to be
A home without love is no home at all
You make rules I follow

Never questioning your actions
And so I give in to you and your every command
You give orders and so I follow
It were your castle

You had all the controlled
You were in command
The place I call home was a torture chamber
Living with you was nothing but grief, hopelessness
The lonely place I call home

This cold place I call home
This place I call home was a home full of Hate, Anger, and rage
A home is not a home without love

ONE DAY

One evening I mad supper, I thought it would be very nice if I made a new dish
for Supper
My husband sat down I brought him his supper
He took one look at his supper and asked me what that is,
Is that what you want to eat?
Before I had a chance to answer him
He began hitting on me and asking me is that's what you want to eat right did
your money buy the food
Get away from me stupid bitch, he began calling me degrading names

AS A MOTHER

As a mother I had to be strong
Gentle, sweet, loving, and understanding
I had to be mother, and father to our daughter
You missed out on so much
You miss out on your daughters first day of school
You missed out on her first grade card
You missed out on the parent teacher meeting
First art mister piece you missed out on her first everything

YOU ARE

You are confusing me
What do you want from me?
Sometimes you can be so nice
And sometimes you can be so abusive and demanding
Why are you doing this?
What are you trying to do to me?
Why are you playing games with my head?
Sometimes you want me in
Sometimes you want me out
What do you really want from me?
You put me down so many times
You paralyzed me with fear
You turn me into a scared little child
You were always using treats on me

IT IS

It is respectful to respect others
It is important to forgive others for the pain they have cause us
It is good to be kind to others
And most of all it is important to love your self
It is very important to love one another
It is most important to heal our heart, mind, body, soul and spirit
It is vital to overcome one's fears
It is vital to listen to one very carefully
It is important to love without judgment
Life is filled with enjoyment and surprises
It is wonderful to be loved by some one

LOVE AND HATE

You love me you hate me
You need me you don't need me
You want me out you want me in
You don't want me to live you but you push me out
You said I was the best thing that happen to you but on the other hand I was
the worst thing that happen to you tell me something Harry which is it
Why do you play with my mind so much
Love and hate don't mix
They don't go well together

I HAVE LEARNED

That before I can fix someone else
I must first fix myself
I have learned
Before I can change someone else
I must first change myself
I have learned
Before I can help someone else
I must first help my self
I have learned before I can love someone else
I must first love myself

THE FEELINGS

The feelings of fear you instilled in me is enough to last a lifetime
The feelings, off pain,
The feelings, off loneliness,
The feelings, off sadness,
The feeling of isolation

The feelings of fear you instilled in me with threats off killing me, with threats
off taking my daughter away from me.
You have stolen everything good in my life and destroyed them.
You have stolen my heart and you broke it into a million pieces

You have stoned myself and destroyed it
You have stolen my soul and you send it into so many different places
You have stolen my spirit and you broke it
You have stolen everything good in my life and smashed them

You have stolen everything that I believe in and destroyed it.
The feeling of fear you instilled in me keep me down, keep me back, keeps me
from moving forward in my life
I just want to have some peace with my self

I just want to have some peace in my soul
I just want to have some stillness in my heart.
I just want to be the person I always wanted to be
I just want to be me

YOU NEED TO

No, more this is not loved,
You need to live your own life
I need to live my own life
You need to go your own way
I need to go my own way
We need to go our own separated ways
This is not love
Love does not hurt
I need to live my own life and so do you
Love does not hurt
Don't tell me that you love me for I know what love is and it does not hurt
This is not love this is controlled, this is abuse, this is not good and it's not for me

HOME

Home should be the place where we should be safe
For some people home is not always a safe place to be
For some people home is like a battlefield
Fighting to stay alive

Fighting to survive
Every day is a struggle sometimes home is not always a peaceful place
Home is not always the place most people want to be

In some homes there are secret crimes going on that are not visible to the human eyes.
Home should be the place where we should feel safe, free and comfortable
Home is the place where we should have friendship, companionship trust, honesty, happiness, joy, peace, warmth, laughter, hugs, kisses, unconditional love, thoughtfulness, gentleness,

Kindness, respect, caring, loyalty, humor
Unfortunately for some people home is not safe
Some home are like a war zone
A home without love is not a home

CONTROLLED

You controlled my every move
You controlled my life
You controlled what I can and cannot do
You controlled whom I can talk to
You controlled my phone calls
You complained about everything
I lost everything and everyone around me because of your controlling behavior
I stopped doing the things I love just to please you and to keep you happy you were never happy any way no matter what I did it was never good enough for you.
You give me dirty looks
You choose my clothing
You choose my shoes
You tell me how I should dress if I don't dress the way you say you would get so mad with me its out of this world to describe
Controlling someone does not work
Controlling someone is not love

YOU USED TRICKS

You used tricks
You used violence
You used force
You played with my emotions

You used emotional blackmail on me to get your way
You used fear to control me
You used manipulation to keep me in checked
You said to me if I love you I would do what you wanted

I would do what you say
I will give you what you wanted
You told me that I was selfish because I did not let you do what you wanted
with my body you get mad with me you lost your temper so badly on me you
curse at me, you yelled at me you

Hit on me you asked me to get out of your bed and out of your room before
you used your feet to kick me out of your bed
And so I did because I did not want you to kick me out of your bedroom.
All this problem because I did not want to have sex with you, you forget one
thing this is my

body it is the only one I have you have no controlled over my body no not any
more you cannot do whatever you want with my body any more
I have the rights to say no
And by the way no means no

If I don't want to have sex with you I have the right to say so
And by the way no means no you bastard
If I don't want to have sex with you I have the right to say no
You don't have the right to force yourself on me

Even if I am your wife no still means no
You have to understand my body is my temple you have no respect for my body
You call me your wife but was I really your wife
Who was I to you?

You wear never pleased with anything that I did no matter what I did you were never satisfied you were always complaining about something,
I know longer have controlled over my own life

YOU CALL ME YOUR WIFE

You call me your wife but was I really your wife
Who am I to you?
You were never pleased with anything that I had done,
No matter what I had done you were never satisfied
You were always complaining about something.
I now longer have controlled over my own life
I now longer have confidence in my self
You stole my life away from me
You robbed me of my energy, my strength, my self- esteem, and my sense
of worth
You suck the life right out of me
You make me feel so undersized
Who am I?
Who am I to you?

GOOD-BYE

To you,
You are out of my life.

Good-bye and go to hell.
You call me stupid.
You call me brainless.
Now who is stupid?

Good-bye sadness,
Good-bye loneliness,
Good-bye hates,
Good-bye isolation,

Good-bye hopelessness,
Good-bye stress,
Good bye-misery,
Good-bye torment,

Good-bye pain,
Good-bye frustration.
Good-bye low self-esteem,
Good-bye fears,

Good-bye anger,
Good-by depressions,
Good-bye crying,
Good-bye foolishness,

YOU HAD YOUR CHANCE

Now it is my chance,
I will not allowed you to treat me this way any more
I will not allow you to control me any more
I will not allow you to abuse me any more

You cannot hurt me any more
You cannot scare me any more
Your tricks don't work on me any more
Your fear tactics don't work anymore on me

I am tired of your aggressive behavior
I am tired of your violence behavior
I am tired of your bad temper
I am tired of your anger towards me

I am tired of your moods
I am tired of your violent temper
I am tired of making excuses for your childish behavior
I am tired of you argumentative behavior

I am tired of your confrontational ways
I no longer have to put up with your provoking actions
I no longer have to put up with your foul language and your insults
I no longer have to accept your behavior I need to be treated with respect

I will not allow you to manipulate me any more
I will not allow you to treat me unkind any more
I will not allow you put me down any more
I will not allow you to call me names any more

I will not allow you to verbally abuse me any more
I will not allow you to be nasty towards me any more
I will not allow you to mistreat me any more
I will not allow you to treat me this way anymore I am tired of hurting
I will not allowed you to abuse me mentally, physical, sexually, and financially
any more, I will not, I will not any more
You had your Chances

I NEED SOMEONE

Someone loving
Someone warm
Someone understanding
Someone romantic

Someone gentle
Someone kind
Someone respectfully
Someone trusts worthy

Someone passionate
Someone honest
Someone kindhearted
Someone loyal

Someone humorous
Someone special
Someone compassionate
Someone pleasant

Someone friendly
Someone straightforward
Someone considerate
Someone dedicated

Someone who will not play silly little games with my heart
Someone who will enjoy being with me
Someone who will be proud of me, and proud to be with me?
Someone who will cuddle up with me on a cold winters day or night

Someone who will listen to me an never be too busy for me
Someone who will appreciate me just as I am
Someone I can share my every thought with
Someone who will communicate well with me

Someone who likes making conversation
Someone who would lift me up and not down
And most of all someone positive and sweet

LOVE IS

Love is pleasant
Love is kind
Love is gentle
Love is warm

Love is sweet
Love is joyful
Love is happiness
Love is patience

Love is kindness
Love is sharing
Love is given not taken
Love is respect

Love is unconditional
Love is tender
Love is not provoked
Love is not put down

Love is a two way street
Love is compassionate
Love is caring
Love is straightforwardness

Love is friendly
Love is genuine
Love is understanding
Love is passionate

Love is openness
Love is humorous
Love is knowing
Love is pure

FIGHTING

Hash words spoken,
Glass got broken,
Glass got smash,
Clothing, got destroy, clothing got cut up, clothing got rip up

Name-calling went back and forth,
Insults went flying back and forth
Doors got slammed
Food went slamming

Slaps went flying
Punch went flying
Child just keeps standing, and then child went crying,
Now longer could the child just stand they looking on

No one stop to comfort the child, but how could we or how could I have
comfort the child when myself was on the bed room floor fighting to stay alive,
fighting for my life, fighting to survive,
Fighting so that I don't lose my life,
Yelling, slapping, cursing, beating and the name-calling went on

It feels like hours
I cannot live like this anymore,
The fighting,
The name calling,

The finger pointing,
The blaming,
The beatings,
The accusation,

The put down,
The manipulation,
It has to stop I cannot take this any more
I cannot live like this any more

Every day is a struggle in my own home not knowing what to expect,
Never knowing what you would do next,
Never knowing,

RECLAIMING MY LIFE

Never knowing,

I can't,
I can't do this any more
I thought of

I thought of disappearing and not telling anyone where I am going,
And not leaving a forward address or a phone number,
And so I have done,
I give you so many chances,

But you never change,
You only cared about your self
You never cared for our daughter or for my self

I was nothing to you, was I?
I did my best, but my best was not my best,
Well I have left, and I have no regrets
I don't even miss you

I don't even think of you
I don't want to see you're revolting face any more
I don't want to see you
I don't want to talk to you

I don't want anything to do with you any more
Go away, and leave me alone
Stay away for good

I HAVE PRAYED

I have pray to God to take me away to day
I pray to God that I am not left in this hell of a life to suffer
I am hurting,
I am in pain,
I am troubled,
I am confused,
I am suffering,
I am sad
I am wounded,
I am mistreated
I am sad
I pray today God take me away today,
Anywhere else would be better than this hell of a place I call home

I HAVE BEEN

I have been beaten down; I have been beaten up,

I have been mistreated; I have been treated like a fool,

I have been treated poorly; I have been treated roughly,

I have been treated disrespected,

I have been treated like an animal in training,

LIFE IS NOT

Life is not what it appears to be
Afraid of you, afraid of what you would do
When things don't go your way, afraid of your reaction
Living with you were like living in hell it self
I walked around being afraid of you
Living with you was always scary, never knowing what to expect from you.
Living with you was like walking on eggshells or broken glasses
Always being careful of what I do or say around you
Never knowing what would happen next
Never knowing when your mood would change
Never knowing whom you would be next
Never knowing when you would lose your temper

NOTHING BUT PAIN

You did what you wanted regardless of the consequences.
You had the right to be angry.
But that don't give you the right to hurt me
Swear at me,
Be cruel towards me,
Hit me,
And beat up on me
That was not the right thing to do to me
Living with you was nothing but heartbreaking, and pain
Nothing but torture, nothing but heartache
You cause me so much sorrow, so much shame and so much pain,

MONTRÉAL

I have to get out of Montreal
I am choking here, I cannot breath
I feel trapped here
I feel chain here

I feel lost here
I feel alone here
No one understand what I am going through
I feel like there is a mad man walking around,

Taunting me,
Haunting me,
Torment me,
Scaring me, and would not stop
Will this ever end?

What do you really want from me?
What scary me the most is that I don't know what you want from me,
When would you ever live me alone?
When would you stop torment me?

When will you stop treating me?
When would you stop torture me?
When would you stop harassing me?
I don't want to die
I have to get out of here I am choking here too much anguish, too much pain,
too much unhappiness too much sadness

I have to get out of Montréal
I feel in prison here

I AM PUZZLED

You continued to insult me
You continued to threaten me
You do whatever you want
You are confusing me

What do you really want from me?
Sometimes you can be so hostile
Why are you doing this?
What are you trying to do to me?

Why are you playing with my head?
Sometimes you want me out, and sometimes you want me in
What do you really want from me?
You put me down so many times

You cripple me with fear
You turned me into a scared little child
You were always using threats on me
Your insults were out of this world

Your words were so aggressively used
Your words were sharp like a knife
Your attacks were so vicious
Never knowing what to expect from you, your moods were like the weather
changing from one to the next

Never knowing which mood you will be in next
You make life so difficult, so hard, and so difficult, for everyone

WHY DO YOU?

Why do you hurt me so?
Only you know why
I may never get an answer
You treat me so badly even when I was good to you
No matter what I did you were never satisfied
You were always finding faults for the smallest things
You made trouble for foolish things
You accuse me of being disloyal
I don't know what you want from me
I give up everything that I was doing for you.
I stopped talking to my friends
I stopped going to church because of you.
No matter what I did you were always accusing me of doing things I know
nothing about

DIRTY LOOKS

The way you look at me my God if looks could killed I would be a dead woman today
You look at me and take deep breaths, making growling sounds or funny noises
You walk so hard I can feel it in my chest or stomach
Living with you was unbearable
If you are not happy, you make sure no one else in the home was not happy to
You blame me for everything that went wrong in your life
Making growling sounds, looking at me nasty, slamming dishes down in the kitchen sink, and walking hard on the floor so that I would feel bad for your unhappiness well it worked and know more will it work

I WAS

I was never comfortable with my self

I was never comfortable with whom I am

I was never comfortable with how I looked

I was never comfortable with the way I dressed

I was never comfortable with my body

I was never comfortable with my nose

I was never comfortable with my mouth

I was never comfortable with my lips

I was never comfortable with my feet

I was never comfortable with the way I looked

I was never comfortable with who I am

Because that how I was made to feel all my life

Do you know, what that was like to be abuse or mistreated by the people who was supposed to love me

Well it happen to me

I WAS TOLD

I was told my smile was too broad
I was told that my mouth was too big
I was told that my lips were too thick
I was told that my breast was too big
I was told that my feet were too big
I was told that my nose was too big
I was told that I was too ugly
I was told that I was too stupid and dunce
Those words I heard over and over as a young girl by my mother
Those words turn me into a very shy person I always thought of myself just the way my mother say it
It took me thirty-eight years to realize that I am a beautiful woman when a social worker took me aside one day

PEACE

I am now at peace with my self
I now have peace within my self
I have peace, and peace have found me.
I have found peace in my heart

I now feel completely at peace with who I am
I now feel that my soul is at peace
I know longer feel frightened
I now longer feel depressed

I know longer feel confused
I know longer have to hide behind lies
I know longer have to be someone I am not
I know longer feel that deep pain in my heart

I BELIEVE

I believe that all human being should respect each other
I believe that every human being should be free
I believe that we all should be able to speak freely
I believe that we should be respectful of each other's space

I believe that we all should all have the same opportunities and chances in life
I believe that everyone should be happy
I believe that everyone should be loved
I believe that everyone should be gentle

I believe that everyone should be kind
I believe that everyone should be respected.
I believe everyone should accept each other just the way they are.
I believe everyone should set boundaries

I believe that everyone should set goals
I believe that everyone should be free from pain
I believe that everyone should be free from hunger
I believe that everyone should have a best friend

I believe that everyone should have a meaningful life
I believe that everyone should love him or her self
I believe that we should not hurt others on purpose
I believe that no one should be beaten

I believe that children should not be strike
I believe that everyone should be accepted
I believe that families should love respect and cherish each other
I believe that everyone should have they own opinion

I believe that everyone should believe in they own destiny
I believe that we should be able to get along
I believe that we have the right to be whom or what we want to be
I believe that we are all unique and special

I believe that we are blessed despite of our struggles and troubles
I believe that everyone should express his or her opinions
I believe that everyone have the right to be treated fairly and equally

I believe that everyone have the right to be treated with compassion and understanding

I believe that we should cherish every moment
I believe that we should not put each other down
I believe that we all do not have the same believes but we must respect, each other's feelings, opinions, spaces, time, and we must be compassion, and understanding to each other

MY LITTLE ANGEL

I am prude to have you in my life,

You have brought me such joy, such happiness

You are the most beautiful person I have ever known

God has blessed me with such a wonderful little gift

What a blessing I have received

What does one do to receive such a blessing?

So pretty, so soft, so gentle, so fragile, and so little

You are my pride and joy

You are so special

You are the most beautiful little person I have ever laid my eyes on

What a blessing you are to me

To my Daughter

I WENT

I went back and forth
Believing in you,
Believing in your lies,
Believing in your craziness,
I feel so mix up,
I feel so empty inside.
I feel so broken hearted,
I feel so confused,
I feel so hopeless,
I feel so hurt,
I feel so miserable,
I feel so angry,
I feel so alone,
You said you cared about me
But why do you hurt me so badly?
Why do you hate me so much?
I am so lost
I put my heart in your hands; you walked all over my heart
You broke my heart so badly

TO MY FRIEND (J)

You are an angel to me
An angel walking on God green pasture
An angel sends straight from heaven
An angel with a big wonderful heart

An angel walking on earth so graceful
An angel of great hopes
An angel of encouragement
An angel of support

An angel of acceptance
An angel with such beauty
An angel with such happiness
An angel with such peace

An angel with such joy
An angel with great understanding
An angel with such love
An angel so sweet and kind

An angel of love
Never will I forget
How wonderful of an angel you have been to me

DREAMING OF

Dreaming of a life without violent
Dreaming of a life without fear
Dreaming of a life of freedom
Dreaming of a peaceful world

Dreaming of a life worth living
Dreaming of a day when they would be no pain in the world
Dreaming of a world where they would be no more discrimination
Dreaming of a world without war

Dreaming of a world without pollution
Dreaming of a world without child hood diseases
Dreaming of a world without suffering children
Dreaming of a world without illness

Dreaming of a world where we can all just sit and watch the sunset in harmony
Dreaming of a world full of compassion
Dreaming of a world with nothing but love for each other
Dreaming of a world with peace

Dreaming of a world where people would do the right thing
Dreaming of a world where they would be no suffering
Dreaming of a world with nothing but respect
Dreaming of a world without struggles

Dreaming of a world without wickedness
Dreaming of a world without humiliation
Dreaming of a world without hostility
Dreaming of a world where people would do the right things

Dreaming of a world without struggles, cruelty, humiliation, sadness, hostility, and without discomfort,
Dreaming of a world without sadness
Dreaming of a world without discomfort
Dreaming of a world full with kindheartedness, and kindhearted people
Dreaming of a better life for you and for me

DON'T KNOW

I don't know who I am any more

I am so lost

Lost somewhere inside myself

I have been lost, lost so long ago

I don't know if I can find my way back

I am so angry

So dam angry

No one knows but me how angry I am feeling

I am angry because you take me for granted

I feel so hollow

I feel like there is an empty space inside of me waiting, waiting to be filled

I feel so alone

I feel like if no one understands me

I feel like if something is wrong with me

I feel like if something is missing

What is my problem?

Why do I feel this way?

Why do I feel like if I am the only person in the world?

I feel very sad and I don't know why

YOU HIT ME

You hit me

You yelled at me

You curse at me

You call me the most degrading names in the book

You call me stupid

You call me ugly

You call me fat

You call me a bitch

You call me a whore

You said I was useless

You said that I sleep like a cow

You call me a stupid cow

And you said that I was nothing

No one wants me

No one love me

You said that I was garbage

So tell me why you want me back

If I am all those things you say I am then tell me something

Why do you want me back in your life?

YOU CALL ME

You call me worthless

I am priceless

You call me stupid

I am smart

You call me useless

I am useful

You call me fat

I am beautiful

You call me a whore

I am a lady

You call me a no body

I am important

I am somebody

You call me ugly

I am adorable

You call me handicap

I am wonderfully made

You call me weak
I am strong

YOU WAS SO CRUEL

You hate with a passion
You set out to hurt me
You set out to destroy my life
You set out to make my life difficult

You destroy things that meant a lot to me
You were always putting me down
You were always yelling at me
You were always cursing at me

You were always calling me degrading names
For you nothing seems right
You made me feel that I was nothing
You made me feel so badly about my self
You call me useless

You call me handicap
Living with you
Was like living in hell
You made me feel fat and ugly

You played with my head, and my mind
I trusted you
With my whole heart, mind, body, and spirit, and my love,

THE BEAUTY OF LIFE

I have found it today
I feel at peace with myself today
I am at one with myself today

The freedom I feel today
The freedom I get today
The warmness I get today
Today I discovered myself

I am at one with nature
Nature is at one with me
Birds singing
Wings flapping

Geese swimming
Ducks quacking
Water flowing

Life is wonderful
And I am a part of it all
The smell of the fresh breeze blowing on my cheeks
The feel of the open air on my face

Trees rocking back and forth
Branches crackling
Leaves flapping in the wind
Sitting here looking around me

Oh so beautiful
Beautiful in every way
Everything around me
Oh so peace full

YOU HATE

You hate me with a passion
You set out to hurt me
You set out to destroy my life
You set out to make life difficult for me
You destroyed things that means a lot to me
You were always putting me down
You were always yelling at me
You were cursing at me
You were always calling me degrading

TAKE

Take responsibilities for your behavior,
Stop blaming others for your troubles
You never take responsibilities for you actions
You never say that you were sorry
For what you have done to us
To me
To your daughter
To your family
It was always someone fault
Someone else problem
You were always blame someone else for your wrongdoing
For your mistakes

I WAS FREE

But not really

Living with you

We're being in a prison

I was not free to express myself

To express my views

To express my feelings

My thoughts or my opinion

I was free but not really

I was not allowed to be myself

I was living someone else's life

I was not allowed to be who I was meant to be

I was being someone else

Because I was not allowed to be myself

WHEN I LET YOU

When I let you have your way

With me or give in to your demands

You would treat me good

But the minute

I say no to you

Or the minute I did not

Do what you want

I am the biggest whore and the biggest bitch in Canada

How can you call me degrading names?

Put me down, swear at me, and then expect me to have sex with you

You are,

You are stupid

You will always be stupid

You hear me

Listen to me and listen very well

You are nothing

You would always be nothing

Stupid whore

Get out of my sight

I HAVE

I have to say that I often thought of

Leaving it all behind

And not looking back

I am

So confused

So depress

So alone

No one really care any way

They see

But there don't see

They here

But there don't here

I don't think they really understand what I am going through

I WANT YOU

I want you to know
That I forgive you
For all the pain you cause me
For all the times you made me cry
For all the times you hurt me
For all the times you cut up my clothing and throw them in the garbage
For hitting me
For calling me degrading names

I DIDN'T MEAN I

I didn't meant anything to you now did I
I think until I cannot think any more
Everything is so mixed up in my head, and in my mind
I am so confused

I cannot think straight any more
I am holding a cup of tea in my hand
Mixed with some pills don't asked what kind or how many
For I don't know and I don't care anymore I made up a mixture

I am ending it all today
I cannot do this anymore
I cannot live like this any more
I don't know what to do any more

They say they are here to help
But when the time comes
To show support
There walked away
There is no one there

No shoulder to lean on
No one to tell me it's ok
Today I am ending it all

I made up a mixture
So many mixed feelings
So many unwanted thoughts

I cannot control them any more
I am ending it all today

YOU

You made an awful mistake

And it cost you your family

And caused so much heartache

You was always so angry

I don't know why

And you want me to stay with you

You don't love me

You made me cry so many times

You made me sad

I felt so empty

Because of your actions

I hope you have learned your lesson now

YOUR

The love we shared in the beginning died half way through

Your values change

Your manner change

Your behavior change

Your attitude change

Your words change

I thought I knew you but really I didn't

I DON'T WANT

We will never get back together

I don't want you in my life anymore

I don't want to get back with you

Stop asking me to come back to you

I don't want to work things out with you any more

I just want out

I had it with your behavior

I had it with your smart remark

I don't want to be your wife any more

You don't care anything about me

You hurt me so many times

I want to be free from you

I want to flush you right out of my system

I DON'T BLAME MYSELF

I don't blame myself any more

For allowing you to mistreated me

Tolerating your behavior

Does not change who I am

Your words once break me down

But today I am strong

Today I am moving on

I want you to know

I am not stupid as you claim

I am not ugly as you claim

I am not a whore as you say

I am not a bitch as you thought

I am not fat as you say

And I am not crazy as you say

I am wonderful

You try to change me

You try to break me

With time I would be completely find again

YOU BEG ME

You beg me to come back home

You beg me to come back to you but I don't think so

You beg me to forgive you

You beg me to give you another chance

I tell you, you must be crazy

You were always accusing me

Always blaming me

Always putting me down

I am sorry I cannot be with you any way

You put me to so much

You treat me like an animal in training

We cannot be together

I don't want to be with you

I don't want to think about you any more

Please don't ask me to come back to you

THIS IS PICTURE

This is a picture of my ex husband
you were like many people in one
Stop with your lies
You cannot forget me good for you

You are not ready to live without me
You need me to survive
You cannot live without me well; well that's a first
Why are you doing this to me

You fucking whore
Nobody want you, you hear me
You cannot do anything for your self
Come home why are you doing this to me

You know I love you
Think about all the things we talked about
Think about all the plans we made
I don't want to be without you

Look at you, you fucking stupid whore
Stupid bitch
Look at you, you handicap
I miss you

I miss being with you
I miss talking with you
You said I don't love you but I do love you
You continued to hurt me

You don't treat me good
You don't treat me right
I don't want to be treated like that any more
I just want to forget this treatment

You fucking stupid whore
Look at you, you stupid bitch
I miss you I miss you
I miss being with you

I miss talking with you
You said I don't love you but I do love you
Why do you want me back?
When you don't get your way

You would become very abusive

MY FRIEND

Today my friend died
Not off a natural cause
Not off ill-health
She died all-alone
On the cold kitchen floor
Of her apartment

She died broken hearted
She died by the hands of the man who claimed to love her
She was stabbed thirty seven times
By the hands of the same man who say he love her

While her four years old child
Lay sleeping in the next room
He said he love her to much to see her with someone else
And that he could not let her go

He calls that love
I call that hate
Hate with a passion

My friends bleed to death
On her cold kitchen floor
She did not have the chance to reach for her telephone
She did not have the chance to call the police

She was someone's daughter
She was someone's mother
She was someone's sister
She was someone' aunty
She was my friend

She was only thirty-seven years old
No one heard her screams for help
No one feel's her pain
No one feel's her sadness

Today my friend died
Hardly anyone notice

She died by the hands of the man
Who claims to love her?

She died of a broken heart
She died a lonely woman
She died a sad death
She died all-alone

She died in her own blood
She died a horrible death
On her kitchen floor
By the hands of the man who claims to love her

To many times woman and men hurt the ones they love

This poem is dedicated to my friend who was stabbed and killed by her husband,
in 1996

MONTRÉAL

I feel trapped here
I feel like if I am in jail here
I have to get out of here
I am chocking here I cannot breath

I feel trapped
I feel chained
I feel like I am in a corner and my back is against the wall
I cannot turn, I cannot, move
No way to turn

I feel lost I feel alone
No one understand how I really feel
No one understand what I am going through

I feel like there is a mad man walking around
Following me,
Tormenting me,
Hunting me,
Chasing me,

Scaring me
Not living me alone
My God
When this will ever end

What do you want from me?
What is scarier about you is that I don't know what you want from me when
will you stop harassing me?
When will you stop threatening me?

You continue to insult me
You continue to make death treats on my life
You always do what you want
What do you really want from me?
Sometimes you can be so nice and sometimes you can be so abusive

Why are you doing this to me?
What are you trying do to to me?

Why are you playing with my heart?
Sometimes you want me in and sometimes you want me out
What do you really want from me?

You put me down so many times
You cripple me with fear
You turn me into something I was not
Always using treats on me

Your insult was too much to take
Your words was aggressive like a lion
Your words cut like a knife
Your attacks was so I aggressive at times it was scary

Never knowing what to expect from you
Your mood was like the weather
Changing from one minute to the next
Never knowing which mood you would be in next

Living with you was very scary
Never knowing when your mood would change
You switch from one mood to the next
You made life so hard, difficult, and unbearable

For every on in the home
Never knowing who you would be next
When will all this end?
Sometimes I think
You will only stop when I am six feet under
It will end

Before that happen
I have to live Montréal
I have to get out of here

FEARING

I have walked away so many times from you
Unsure of what life would be like without you
Unsure of what the future holds for me

Fearing of the unknown
Fearing of what is out there
Fearing of facing life alone
Fearing of facing life without you

So many times we been back and forth
So many times you lost your temper
So many times you get angry with me

So many times I have walked away from you
Yet still I always retune
Retune to what I really don't know why
Nothing ever change
Things still remain the same

You feed me with broken promise
And each time I fall for it
Your sweet words I fall for it
Your charms I fall for it

THINGS

Things will always go wrong in our lives, and in our relationship

Life will hit us with twist and turns

Life has many ups and down

Life has its much trouble

And it's an up hills battle

Sometimes we get stock

And sometimes we get unstuck

And sometimes we walked away freely

But we don't have to abuse the ones we love

No matter what curve ball life throws at us

We will come out on top

COMPASSION

To be compassion means to love
To be compassion means to be able to listen with both ears
To be compassion means to be able to understanding someone feelings
To be compassion means to be respectful

To be compassion means to be able to say I am sorry
To be compassion means to be gentle
To be compassion means to be able to share your heart with someone else
To be compassion means to be able to give a hug to a friend in need

To be compassion means to go for a walk with friends who need someone to
talk to
To be compassion means to be able to say to a friend you need a break i will take
you the movies my treat
To be compassion is to be able to say to a friend I will take care of the children
take a breather you deserved one
To be compassion means to be able to say thank you for coming to my rescue

To be compassion means to be able to say I appreciate your presence in my life
To be compassion means to say I appreciate your friendship
Be compassion in all you do

POSITIVE

I began thinking positive
I began feeding my mind, my body, and soul with positive thoughts
I began thinking good thoughts about my self
I now find the goodness in my life and in myself

I began to open my heart to new things
I began to appreciate the greatness of life
I began to take time for my self
I began to heal my heart

I stop feeling guilty for things I had no controlled over
I began tell myself that I am special
I began telling myself that I am wonderful and beautiful
I began telling myself that there is no one quite like me

I began to love myself unconditionally
I now began to appreciate my self
I am now my best friend you know the kind of friend that would always be

They're for you any time day or night for you come rain, sun, winter, snow,
The kind of friend that would treat you with gentleness, kindness, and who would be sweet,

Warm, loving, and special give you respect and reach out to you in time of needs
The friend who would tell you
How extraordinary
How unique

How wonderful
How courageous
How strong and understanding you are
That's the kind of friends I am to myself today

SOMETIMES

Sometimes some people come into our lives and they leaves such an in
Print on our lives that would make us think that life is wonderful and sweet
Sometimes those people stay in our live and sometime they just pass through
And sometimes we don't get to say to those people thank you
For helping change our life or thank you for helping me see things clearly in
my life
Thank you for just being there
Thank you so much.

PEOPLE

In my life I have meet many wonderful people with big hearts

People who are willing to give and not take

People who are willing to listen and not talked over you

People who are really caring

People who truly love

People who fantastically understand

People who would always be there comes rain or shine

People who would always be there with an encouraging word and would always have a word of encouragement for you

People you can always count on

People who would always be there with open arms and open hearts

GET IN TOUCH

Get in touch with whom you are

And you are special just remember that

There is no one quite like you

Enjoy your life

This life is the only one you got

Live your life honestly and respectfully

I know longer have to wonder

What might have been?

Or what could have been

Because I have controlled over my life today

YOU HIT ME

You yelled at me
You curse at me you call me the most degrading names in the book
You call me stupid, ugly, fat, bitch, whore, handicap,
You said I sleep like a cow
You call me garbage
So tell me something if you say I am all those things, you say I am then tell me
why do you want me back in your life?
What do you want with me?

I HAVE LEARNED

I have learned
For one to truly be happy
One must first love one self
One must learned to let go
Of all the hurt, pain, sadness, and anger
One must learn to forgive
One must truly find contentment in one's life and in one self
Only then can one truly find inner peace
And only then can one truly be happy
I have learned that I cannot
Undo the past
But I can work on the present and move on
I cannot undo what has been done in my life,
But I can make changes in my life
And In my attitude

AS WOMEN

As women we should be treated with the utmost respect
As women we should be treated
Like mothers,
Like daughters,
Like aunties,
Like sisters,
Like grandmother,
Like friends,
As mothers we should be given the respect we deserved

I HAVE LIVED

I have lived in a silent world
For far too long
I have cried in silence for far too long
I have been sad for far too long
Now it is time for me to move on with my life

THINGS

Things will always go wrong in our lives
Life will hit us with twists and turns
Life has its many ups and downs
Life has its many bumps

Life has its much trouble
Life has its many up hills battles
Sometimes we may get stuck

And sometimes we walk away freely
Sometimes we may not have food to put on our table to feed our children and
love one
Sometimes we may want thing
But we cannot afford it
That means we have to worked harder to get it

Life is sometime not fair
Sometimes life can be depressing
Sometimes life can be hard
Sometimes life does not work out the way we plan it

Don't give up hang in tight
Never give up never quit
Be tuff and that know you are strong
Don't let anyone say on to you any more

YOU LOST

You lost controlled over my life

You no longer
Have controlled over my life any more
You no longer have controlled over my thoughts
You no longer have controlled over my emotion

YOU MISSED OUT

You missed out on so much

You missed out on your daughter's first day of school

On her first parent teacher meeting

On her first grade card

You miss out on so much

You missed out on the first everything in your daughter's life

What a lost for you

That did not have to happen

But it did

You missed out on so much

I AM

I have been empty as a shell for a very long time

I have been hollow as a box

I have been what you wanted me to be, not any more

Now I have found myself and I like what I have found

I am what I say I am today

Not what you say I was yesterday

And not what you say I am any more

You cannot dictate my life any more

I am the driver of my life not you any more

I am in charge of my life not you

You had you doing and saying for a very long time in my life

Not any more I am taking back controlled

I am taking controlled of my life

You cannot command me any more

You cannot controlled me any more

You cannot manipulate me any more

You cannot break me down any more

No, no, no,

WHY DO YOU?

Why do you hate me so much?
Why do you hurt me so?
Only you know why
Or maybe not

I may never know why or get an answer
You treat me so badly
Even when I was good to you
You were very horrible to me

No matter what I did
You were never content
You find fault for the smallest things that I did
For example I put my handbag on the kitchen table

To give our daughter a glass of milk
You got so angry
And created a problem
For what I don't know

You make problems for stupid things
You accused me of fucking around on you
You accused me of bringing men in your house when you are not there
I could not go any way or do anything without you accusing me

I don't know what you really want from me any more
I give up everything for you
I stop going to church for you
I give up my friends for you

I stop going to the library for you
But you still complained
What more do you want from me
I don't have anything more to give to you

I don't know what to do any more
I cannot please you
You just keep putting me down, bringing me down
No matter what I did you complained

YOU

You cheated me of my happiness
You made my life so miserable
You cause me so much anguish
You cause me so much stress
You cause me so much heartache
You cause me so much grief
You cause me so much unhappiness
You cause me so much suffering
You cause me so much agony
You cause me so much discomfort

MY STRENGTH

My strength is gone
I can no longer fight you any more
I am afraid to fight back
I am no longer able to fight back
I have not much energy left
I have no more tears to fall

LOVE

Love cannot be force
Love does not force itself on anyone
I cannot force you to love me
You cannot force me to love you
I am the only me there will ever be
I have learned that I must first love myself
Before I can first love anyone
Loving myself is the most important thing I can do for myself
And the best thing I can do for myself
I have learned that I am number one
And I am important

TODAY I AM

Today I am free to be myself
Today I can walk without being afraid
Today I am free because someone listens to me
Today I am free because someone believe in me
Today I am free because some cared and love me
Thank you,

I CANNOT DO ANYTHING

I am sick and tired of your complaining
I cannot do this any more
You are always doing and saying horrible things to hurt me
Treating me as if I am a nobody
That was not the right to do

YOU REFUSE

You refuse to take advice from me
You refuse to listen to me
You told me that you would never take advice from bitch of a woman like me
You asked me why you have to take advice from a woman
Dam piece of shit woman like me
Stupid bitch like you
Well if you did not notice I am not just any woman I am your wife

I AM SICK AND TIRED

I am sick and tired of your accusations
I cannot do anything without your horrible remarks
You were always doing and saying degrading things to me
I cannot do anything without you accusing me

THE LOOK

The look you give to me when you are mad and upset
The look in your eyes
The look on your face
The language you speak
The tone in your voice
The vain on your face and neck pops out
You swelled up like a porcupine
You call me degrading names
And you expect me to make love to you
Well what you think of me
You call me a bitch
I maybe a bitch
But I am not your bitch
I don't want your filthy hands touching on me any more
I will never let you touch me any more
This body belongs to me
But you act like if I am a piece of property
Well I am not
This body is the only one I have and I have to take care of it

WHY DO YOU

Why do you laugh at me in my sadness?

Why do you make fun at me?

Why did you have to break up the family?

Why do you laugh at me when I am hurting?

Why do you make fun at me?

Why do you hurt me so?

Why do you laugh at me?

You ripped my heart out

And you trample on it

You watch me hurting

I think you enjoy watching me in pain

TODAY I WAS ASKED

Today I was asked what wrong with my face

How did you get that bruised, I straight-faced lied?

I fell down the steps while doing the laundry and I bruised myself

I am tired of the lies

I am tired of making excuses

I am tired of making excuses for why there are marks on my body

I am tired of making excuses for your behavior

I am tired of pretending

That enough I had it

I cannot do this anymore

THE GRAVE

The grave was open
Waiting for
Me to fall in
Waiting for me to give up
The grave was set for me
Waiting to swallow me up
But not today

DEPRESSION

Depression is a silent killer
Depression eats away at your inner self
Depression makes a person feel lonely
Depression makes a person feels alone

Depression makes a person feels helpless
Depression makes a person feels hopeless
Depression makes a person feels tired
Depression makes a person feels like there in a silent world of their own

Depression makes a person lose interests
Depression makes a person think that life is not worth living
Depression makes a person worry over the smallest things
Depression makes a person feels nervous

Depression makes a person have problems concentrated
Depression rob a person of their energy
Depression makes a person lose their apatite
Depression makes a person feels like crying all the time

Depression makes a person feels confused
Depression makes a person feels confused
Depression makes a person lose their memory

Depression makes a person thinks Suicidal thoughts
Depression makes a person feels like dying

Depression makes a person feels worthless
Depression makes a person feels helpless
Depression makes a person feels self-hatred

Depression makes a person feels lost
Depression can knock one down really hard

SLEEPLESS NIGHTS

Silent cries
You were very frightening to me
your Panic and rage got the best of you
Day after day

I try to put up with your behavior
I try to fight you of
I try to stay alive
I am tired of fight you off of me

I am tired of fighting with you
you let your rages controlled you
you let your rage got the best of you
Your rage and anger make you lost your family

Your anger makes you lose controlled
Rage and anger destroy your family
Too much pain
Too many sleepless nights

Too many tears fall
I did everything to please you
I stop talking to my friends
Stop going to church

Everything I enjoyed doing
I just stop because you keep accusing me
Of things I don't know anything about
But you was never happy

You always find fault
You were always complain over nothing

MY SELF-ESTEEM

My self-esteem took a nosedive
You bring me down so low,
You break me down to nothing,
I believe in everything you told me
You said
I was good for nothing
Stupid,
Fat,
Ugly,
Useless,
Handicap,
Whore,
Bitch,
Nothing,

BLAMING

You blame me for everything
For your mood
For your anger
For your temper
Things you should take responsibility for, you blame me for them
You blame me for all the things you have done wrong
and for everything that went wrong in your life

I GIVE

I loved you so much
I give my whole self to you
I give my whole heart to you
You had my whole heart
And you crushed my heart into little bits and pieces like crackers,
I was so in love with you and you knew it I am sure
But you took me and my love for granted
You played with my mind
You played with my emotion
You treat me like a fool
You had my heart in the palm of your hands and you squeeze the life right out
of it you didn't not even try to protect my heart
You crushed it along with my love for you

CHILDREN

Children need to be loved unconditionally
Children need to be respected
Children need to be treated with respect
Children need to be appreciated

Children need to be understood
Children need to be taken seriously
Children need to be treated like children

Children need to be encouraged
Children need to be protected
Children need to be praised
Children need to be acknowledged

Children need to feel wanted
Children need to be treated with firmness
Children need to love them self
Children need to love who they are

Children need to be safe
Children need to be cherish
Children need to be listen too
Children need to feel important

Children need to be cared for
Children need to be accepted
Children need to be treated fairly
Children need to be free to choose

MY HOME WAS A SAD PLACE TO BE

Many times I thought of running away
Just living, just go somewhere where no one knows me
But it was easy to think about it than to do it
Your jealousy is getting out of controlled
Your violent behavior is scary
You are always yelling and swearing at me
Always blaming me

YOU BLAME ME

You said I make you hit me
I made you yelled at me
I made you cut up my clothing's
I made you take things away from me

I make you throw my belongings in the garbage
I made you pushed me out of the house and closed the door
Grow up be a man stop blaming me
I am tired

Take responsibility for your actions stop,
I could not make you do anything
Even if I try so why are you blaming me?
I am not the one that got angry

I am not the one who starts cutting up things that don't belong to me
I am not the one who put things in the garbage that don't belong to me
I am not the one, who starts hitting on you,
You hit me because you wanted to hit me

Not because I made you hit me
You hit me and blame me for hitting me
You say I made you angry
How did I made you angry really I wish you could stop blaming me for your mistakes

And start taking responsibility for your actions
You did what you wanted to do
Now stop blaming me
You played with my mind

I believed in you
I trusted you
I loved you
And most of all I trusted you with my heart

And you played on my love for you
You keep on hurting me over and over again
I don't know how I allowed you to treat me that way
I don't know how I stayed so long with you

Eight and a half years can you imagine that?
Some people say I was crazy to stay with you so long
I don't think I was crazy
I loved you

What did I get for loving you heart ache and pain I was confused to think that
you would change
Confused by the fact that I can love someone like you
Someone who will never change
Confused with the thought that I married someone like you

I cannot wait to get away from you
you playing a confusing game with me
what make things more confusing for me is that I love you
And that you never changed

HOME

Home should be the most comforting place to be
Home is built upon love and trust
Home is where one's love shines and blossom
Home is where one have laughter and joy
Home is where one find contentment
Home is where one feels safe and secure
Home is where we all come together
Home is where one builds strong relationship
Home is where one feels warm and comfortable
Home is where one builds closeness and bonds
Home is where love one connect with each other
Home is where one fine companionship
Home is where one finds togetherness
A home represent love
Unfortunately for some people home is a horrible place to be sometimes
Home is an unhappy place to be sometimes
Home is a lonely place for one to be sometimes
Home is an unpleasant place to be sometimes
For some people home is lacking love, compassion and friendship
For some people Home is a horrible place to be sometimes
Home is an unhappy place to be sometimes
Home is a lonely place for one to be sometimes
For some people home is lacking love, compassion and friendship

SADNESS

I don't know how to feel any more
My Mind is so confused
I am tired of worrying
I am tired of wondering
My eyes is weaken from crying
I am tired from sleepless nights
I am weaken from lots of appetite
I am tired of feeling fear
I don't know what to do anymore
This is crazy I cannot live like that any more
I am sad
I am tired
I am lost

I LOSE

I lose myself bit by bit

I live day by day

Minute by minute

I was a prisoner in

My own home

In my relationship

Trapped, trapped that's what I felt

I was not living

I was just surviving

BROKEN

Broken heart
Broken dreams
Broken promise
Broken home
Broken life
Broken vows

I HATE

I hate how you come into my life and turn my life upside down
I hate the fact that I let you hurt me
I hate this person you have turn me into
I hate who I have become

I hate what I have become
I hate how angry I have become toward you
I hate the pain you put me true
I hate the pain I cause our daughter

I hate how you never appreciate me for me
I hate how terrible you make me feel about myself
I hate how small you make me feel about myself
I hate how you took my love and turn it into hate

I hate what you make of me
I hate how you make me feel about myself
I hate the way in which you were always complain
I hate the way in which you criticize me all the time

I hate the way you look at me with hate in your eyes
I hate the things you say to me
I hate how you beat on me
I hate the things you did to my mind

I hate how you made me feel fearful all the time
I hate how fat, ugly, stupid, useless, unloved, ashamed, alone and unsafe you make
me feel about my self
I hate the ugly thoughts you put in my mind about myself
I hate the fact that you put hate in me towards you

WHY

Why do you hurt me so
what have I done to you my love
why do you hate me so much
Why are you so angry with me?
Why do you yell at me?
Why do you beat on me?
Why do you use foul language to me?
Why are you so rude to me?

SO MUCH

So much anger
So much hate
Anger that destroys family
Anger that destroys relationship
You let your anger take over your life
Take controlled of your life
Take control over your mouth

I TRY

I try my hardest
To please you
But you just keep hurting me over and over again
And putting me down
You crushed my spirit
You crushed my self-esteem
You crushed my self-confidence
You crushed my believe
I believe in you
But you let me down
Over and over again

I stay up at night time thinking about nothing, nothing at all

My mind went blank at times

And very confused

I feel as if I am living in a crazy world

And living a crazy life

I feel like if I am in a dream and cannot wake up

Death was near
Death was upon me
The grave was open for me
Thinking this is the end for me
I remember thinking this is the end for me
This is my last breath
This is the end for me I am done
I am finish
I am taking my last breath
Kill me I don't care anymore
What more can you do to me
What more can you take from me
There is nothing left of me anymore
You continue choking me
Choke me tighter
Squeeze tighter
Squeeze a little more
What are you waiting for?
Kill me
Kill me already
I don't care ant more
I am already dead

RESPECT

Respect we don't have to like each other but we have to respect each other
Respect is not taken but earn
When you give respect, you will receive respect in retune
You have to give, respect to get respect
Respect is something that has to be earn
You must first learn to respect yourself before you can began to respect others,
Respect is not taken by force
You don't have to yell and swear to get respect
You don't have to be loud or rude to get respect
If you show respect to the people around you believe me you will be respected back

AGAIN

You getting angry again
What set you off this time?
I don't know but I will find out very soon
Just before I can finish my thought
I received a blow to the face
Why I don't know
I will find out in a minute
Words came at me like a weapon
Shaper than a two edge sward
Whoever say words don't hurt
There did not know what they were talking about

I WILL

I will not die today
I will choose to live
I will not live in fear any more
I will choose to live in freedom
I choose to live my life without violence
I choose to live a long lovingly and peacefully life
I will not allow you to treat me like that anymore
I deserved to be respected
I am not your punching bag
I am putting an end to this madness today
I am a human being
Stop, just stop
I had it with you
I am finish

TELL ME

Tell me something why do you want me to be someone else
Don't you think I am beautiful being myself?
Why are you trying to change me?
Why do you want me to be someone else Tell me why
Why do you want me to be someone I am not?
I am wonderfully and beautifully made in the image of God
Don't try to change me

MY SELF-ESTEEM

My self-esteem took a nosedive
I felt so bad about myself
I had no self-self-confidence
I was this shy, silly person,
I just keep choosing friends, and men who took me for granted
I deserved better than that
I can image
Being told things about myself and believing it
I know that sounds crazy but it is very true
At a very young age I was told some degrading things
About myself and I believe it
Especially since it came from my mother
I believe every word she told me about myself
She was my mother and if she said it is true
Mothers don't tell lies to their children now do they
All the things I was told about myself
As a child by my mother I believed it
Growing up I never felt comfortable about my self
I hardly open my mouth to talk,
I never speak up for myself as a child or in my adult life
Every time someone asked me a question I would not answer him or her
I had no confidence in my self
I had no self-esteem

I FEEL SAD

I wish I could disappear
I need to escape this unhappiness
I want to end this sadness I am feeling inside of me
I want to set myself free from this torment
I need to be set free from this feelings I am feeling

I AM

I am loved
I am special
I am wonderful
I am beautiful
I am smart
I am kind
I am gentle
I am excellent
I am loving
I am Thoughtful
I am Considerate
I am Pleasurable
I am Important
I am thankful
I am Grateful
I am amazing
I am sweet
I am not what you say I am
I am what I say I am

GOOD-BYE

Good -bye, good-bye my past
I don't know what tomorrow brings
But for today I am free
Free as I can be
I can be the person I was meant to be
I will become the person
I was meant to be
Some people say that love is blind
But for some people
Love can be dangerous and deadly
And I truly meant deadly
We took an oat
When we got married
Saying till death do we part?
For some people
That oat is taken to heart

YOU DAMAGE MY

My Heart
My soul
My body
My mind
My ways of thinking
My self-esteem
The way I see people
My outlook on life
You turn me into something and someone I was not
You turned me into a liar
A sneaky person
So much distrust
So much anger
I had to hide to talked my friends and to see my friends
You cause me so much hurt

SOMETIMES I CRY

Sometime I cry when I remember
The pain you put me through
Sometimes I cry for my broken heart
Sometimes I cry for my broken spirit
Sometimes I cry for my broken soul
Sometimes I cry for my wounded body
Sometimes I wonder why do you had to be so horrible to me
Sometimes I wonder why did you had to treat me the way you did
Sometimes I wonder why you hurt me so badly
Sometimes when I remember the pain you put me through
I just have to cry and asked myself why
But there are no answers
Just questions that's all there is questions

MY LOVE

I don't think you know how much you really meant to me
You have touched my heart in a very special way
When you embrace me with your soft and gentle hands
I melt like butter
You filled my life with your sweet love
My world become your world
Your world become my world
To my daughter

YOU

You promise to love me
But you give me hated
You swear to cherish me
But you lied
You promise to take care of me in good times and bad times
In sickness and in health
Instead you try to killed me a slow and silent

I AM NOT

I am not stupid
I am not a bitch
I am not a whore
I am not ugly
I am not stink
I am not fat
I am not a loser
I am not who you say I am
I am not what you say I am
Who you say I am don't matter any more
I am not define by the words you say about me
I am much, much more than you will ever know
I am not define by the names you call me
I am not define by what you say about me
I am wonderful, beautiful and smart

I was a mess
I felt so empty and alone
I had to be strong for my daughter's sake
I did my best
I give my all
I have learned to adjust myself to fit the saturation
I have learned my place in the house and in the relationship
I have learned to please my husband
I have learned to do things to please him
I have learned how to not make him angry
I have learned when to speak in my own home
I have learned to be someone I was not
I have learn how to pretend
I knew my place

I THOUGHT ALL THOSE THINGS

Where could I go?
Who could I tell?
Who could I turn to?
Who would believe me?
How stupid would I look?
How stupid would I sound?
Why would anyone believe me?
Why would anyone help me?
Why did you stay with him?
You must like it when he beat up on you
You must like it when he yelled at you
You must like it when he calls you names
You must like it when he swears at you
No one would understand my situation
They would think it's my fault
My husband says I make him do those things to me because I am stupid
They would think I am stupid to
They would think I asked for it
Maybe I am as stupid as he said I am
Who would think such a nice man abuse me?
Why would anyone listen to me?
No one would really understand my problem any way
They would take my daughter away from me
Everyone would think I am crazy
Any way I feel crazy so who wouldn't think that I am crazy
I can lose my daughter if I tell someone

REMEMBER

You swear in court you never hit or abuse me
You did all the things I said you did to me
I did not make anything up
And you know it
You know what you did to me

In our home
Why don't you tell the truth for once in your life?
You know what you did to me over the years
You remember how you talked to me in public

While strangers look on giggle and laugh
You remember that Christmas I made such a wonderful dinner you sat down
and eat your dinner, and then you throw mine in to the garbage
You remember the time you throw food on me

You remember the times you beat up on me
You remember the times you yelled at me
You remember the times you swears at me
You remember the time you pushed me down fifteen flights of steps

You remember the times you bite me on my hand
Remember the times you threatened to end my life
Remember the times you threatened to take my daughter an send her to
your country,
Remember the times you tell me I will not see my daughter any more

You remember the times you tell me you would make my daughter have no
respect for me,
You remember the times you took all my money
You remember the times I had to ask you for money
You remember the many times you ask me what I need money for

You remember you choose my clothing for me when we went shopping
And if I did not like what you choose you would take my hand bag live me with
no money to get home do you remember now
You remember the time you cut up all my important documents

You remember sure you remember stop pretending
Stop telling people you never did those things to me
I did not make those things up
They really happen

And it happen to me
And you did it
I am no longer live in your home any more
Stop making me think that I am crazy

You made me feel that way when I was living with you
No more, no more
I am not crazy
And I am not stupid

Your behaviours has affected our daughter

I AM

I am tired of being haunted by your Beatings
I am tired of being tormented by your swearing and yelling
I am tired of being a slave to Fear
I am tired of shedding tears
I am tired of feeling Sadness
I am tired of feeling depress
I am tired of sleepless nights
I am tired of feeling guilty
I am tired of feeling stupid
I am tired of feeling this small
I am tired of lying
I am tired of covering up for you
I am tired of the blame game
I am tired of the beatings
I am tired of the yelling
I am I tired of the swearing
I am tired of being manipulated
I am tired of being accused
I am tired of wasting my time and energy on you
I am tired, I am tired

NO MORE

No more pain
No more sadness
No more depression
No more lies
No more loneliness
No more tears
No more manipulations
No more beatings
No more yelling
No more swearing
No more if you love me
No more I love you that why
No more mind games
No more guilty feelings
No more confusion
No more craziness
No more feeling stupid
No more fear
No more feeling degrading
No more put downs
No more torment
No more feeling crazy
No more feeling small
No more feeling degraded me in the present of my daughters
No more feel fear to go to bed at night
No more fear to speak for myself any more
No more mess in my life
No more negativity
No more toxic relationship
No more dis-believe
No more destructive behaviour
No more disappointments
No more helpless
No more blaming
No more complaining
No more dishonesty
No more wondering
No more argument

DID YOU REALLY

Did you really think that I cannot do anything without you; you are so very wrong? I don't need you to always tell me what I should do I don't need you to always choose my clothing, my shoes or tell me how I should style my hair, how I should put my make up on, you took it upon yourself to do those things because you said that I was stupid, I was not stupid I was scared of you so badly, and also to keep peace in the home I did what you wanted me to do because when you did not get your way you would make life un- bearable for our daughter and for myself in the home you would destroyed my things, you would break my things, you would cut up my clothing, you would yelled at me, swear at me, shout out degrading things to me, call me degrading names, there was no need for those things I am capable of doing things for myself and by myself, look at me now I am fine since I left you I am doing quite well I went back to school I am now working and I am taking very good care of my daughter and myself I don't need you now do I, I don't need you to hold my hands I have never need you to hold my hands you took it upon yourself it was not because you love me as you claim but because of your controlling behavior , today I am a much stronger, happier, confident person, I am not scared to express my thought's or say what's on my mind I am me again, I am myself again, I am the person you try so hard to breakdown and destroyed over the past eight years I am still standing stronger and standing stronger than before what you did to me was not love, you call that love I have news for you that was hate, hate with a passion

LIVING WITH

Living with you was like living in a war zone
Never knowing when the next bomb would drop
Living with you was like walking on eggshells
Living with you
Was like walking on broken glass

You were like loose cannon
Living with like living with a crazy person
Why did you say horrible things to me?
What was scary about you actions?
Was that you would always lose your temper
In the presence of our daughter

You had no respect for our daughter for yourself for me and for our home
You were a very difficult man to deal with and to live with
Sometimes you would get out of controlled so badly
You could not even stop your self

The vain on your forehead would pop right out your head
Your breath would smell so badly it was unbearable
The Solver from your mouth would fly all over my face
Why did you make yourself so angry?

MY THOUGHT I KEEP TO MY SELF

Any way no one really listen to me
Pretending to be happy
I must go on
Life must go on
I have to survive
I must stay strong
I must not let you see
That I am weak
There are times when I wanted to disappear

I NEED TO BE

I need to be free
I need to have freedom in my life
I need not be limited
I need not be chained
I don't recognized who I am any more
I feel so are shame
So ugly
So useless
So stupid
So unloved
So alone
So lonely
So depressed

I DON'T KNOW

I don't know who I am any more
I am so lost
Lost somewhere inside my self
I have been lost, lost so long ago
I don't know if I can find my way back

I am so angry
So dam angry
No one but me know how angry I am feeling
Everyone takes me for granted

I feel so hollow
I feel like there is an empty space inside of me
Just waiting to be filled
I feel so alone

I feel as if no one understands me
Feeling so alone
Feeling like something is wrong with me
I feel like if something is missing in my life

What is my problem?
Why do I feel like I am the only person in the world?
I feel very sad and I don't know why

I AM TIRED

I am tired of all the fighting
I close my eyes
And I try to forget the past, pain words
I try to forget the frightening and horrible words you said to me
You hurt me tremendously
You almost destroyed me
You killed me a very slow death on the inside
You take away my happiness
My joy, my peace, and my freedom
All you give to me was sorrow, pain sadness,
And you show me hate and anger

LOVE DOES NOT HURT

Love does not hurt
And love is not something that hurts
But why do you hurt me so
Love should not be painful

When someone loves you
They don't hurt you
When you love someone you don't hurt them
When you love someone or someone love
You should love each other unconditionally

Love should be something warm and comforting
Loving someone should be genuine
And it should come for from the heart
As genuine as the love Jesus have for you and I

Loving someone should not be painful
Love does not hurt
Love is not abuse
If someone abuse you and tell you that he or she love you that

Is not love say good-bye
Because things would only get worst
Love is not painful
We should not allowed anyone to abuse us and to hurt us
Love is not abuse

Love does not hurt
When love hurts
It is time to say good-bye
It is time to get out and get some help

CRYING

Crying is the only thing
I can do to make my self-feel better
I am in pain and I don't know why

I feel sad
I feel down all the time
I don't understand what
Is happening to me

Why am I feeling like this?
Why do I feel like if?
I am the only person in the world
Why do I feel so alone?

I Thank God for my daughter
What would I have done?
Without my daughter
By my side
If it was not for my daughter I would of crumble up a long time and die

NO ONE

No one deserve to be abused
In any way shape or form
Hurting me is not the way to get attention
Hurting me would not do anyone any good
If you don't love me

Just let me go my own way
Don't hurt me there is no need for such treatment
Telling me that you love me then you turn around
And hurt me don't make any sense at all to me
Stops treating me like an object
And give me the respect that I deserved

How can you say you love me, and you want me in your life?
And you hurt me in such a horrible way
You cause me so much pain,
So much grief,
Why, tell me why you treat me that way

Why can we just go our own separate way?
We cannot pick up spilled milk
There is no respect here
Live things alone
We need to move on with our lives

There is someone out there just for you
Someone who would understand you and all your hobbits
And behaviors
I am tired of being your
Escape goat not any more

AS WOMEN

As women we should be respected
As woman we should be respected for the love we provide and share
As woman we should be respected for the friends we are
As women we should be respected for our kindheartedness
As women we should be respected for the Sweet smile we give
As women we should be respected for the guidance we give
As woman we are the sunshine that shine so bright in our family,
As woman we should be respected because we are the glue that keeps our family together
As women we should be treated with respect for the mothers, daughter, sister, Aunts, friend and Grandmother we are
As woman we should be respected because we are the glue that holds the family together
As woman we should be respected for the comfort we give to our love ones
As woman we should be respected for the gentle creature we are

I FEEL SAD

I wish I could disappear
I need to escape this unhappiness
I want to end this sadness I am feeling inside of me
I want to be set me free me from this torment
I need to be set free from this feelings I am feeling

I AM

I am loved
I am special
I am wonderful
I am beautiful
I am smart
I am kind
I am gentle
I am excellent
I am loving
I am Thoughtful
I am Considerate
I am Pleasurable
I am Important
I am thankful
I am Grateful
I am amazing
I am sweet

GOOD-BYE

Good –bye, good-bye my past
I don't know what tomorrow brings
But for today I am free
Free as I can be
I can be the person I was meant to be
I will become the person
I was meant to be
Some people say that love is blind
But for some people
Love can be dangerous and deadly
And I truly meant deadly
We took an oat
When we got married
Saying till death do we part?
For some people
That oat is taken to heart

SOMETIMES I CRY

Sometime I cry when I remember
The pain you put me through
Sometimes I cry for my broken heart
Sometimes I cry for my broken spirit
Sometimes I cry for my broken soul
Sometimes I cry for my wounded body
Sometimes I wonder why do you had to be so horrible to me
Sometimes I wonder why did you had to treat me the way you did
Sometimes I wonder why you hurt me so badly
Sometimes when I remember the pain you put me through
I just have to cry and asked myself why
But there are no answers
Just questions that's all there is questions

YOU

You promise to love me
But you give me hated
You swear to cherish me
But you lied
You promise to take care of me in good times and bad times
In sickness and in health
Instead you try to killed me a slow and silent death

I AM NOT

I am not stupid
I am not a bitch
I am not a whore
I am not ugly

I am not stink
I am not fat
I am not a loser
I am not who you say I am

I am not what you say I am
Who you say I am don't matter any more
I am not define by the words you say about me
I am much, much more than you will ever know

I am not define by the names you call me
I am not define by what you say about me
I am wonderful, beautiful and smart

I was a mess
I felt so empty and alone
I had to be strong for my daughter's sake
I did my best
I give my all
I have learned to adjust myself to fit the saturation
I have learned my place in the house and in the relationship
I have been taught that I have to please my husband
I have learned to do things to please him and to do things his way or the high way
I have learned how to not make him angry
I have learned when to speak in my own home
I have learned to be someone I was not
I have learn how to pretend
I knew my place in our Home in our marriage and in our relationship

I THOUGHT ALL THOSE THINGS

Where could I go?
Who could I tell?
Who could I turn to?
Who would believe me?
How stupid would I look?
How stupid would I sound?
Why would anyone believe me?
Why would anyone help me?
Why did you stay with him?
You must like it when he beat up on you
You must like it when he yelled at you
You must like it when he call you names
You must like it when he swears at you
No one would understand my situation
They would think it's my fault
My husband says I make him do those things to me because I am stupid
They would think I am stupid to
They would think I asked for it
Maybe I am as stupid as he said I am
Who would think such a nice man would abuse me?
Why would anyone listen to me?
No one would really understand my problem any way
They would take my daughter away from me
Everyone would think I am crazy
Any way I feel crazy, and they wouldn't think that I am crazy to
I can lose my daughter if I tell someone what's going on in my home

REMEMBER

You swear in court you never hit or abuse me
You did all the things I said you did to me
I did not make anything up
And you know it
You know what you did to me
In our home
Why don't you tell the truth for once in your life?
You know what you did to me over the years
You remember how you talked to me in public
While strangers look on giggle and laugh
You remember that Christmas I made such a wonderful dinner you sat down and eat your dinner, and then you throw mine in to the garbage
You remember the time you throw food on me
You remember the times you beat up on me
You remember the times you yelled at me
You remember the times you swears at me
You remember the time you choke me so hard I could not talk for weeks
You remember the time you pushed me down fifteen flights of steps
You remember the times you bite me on my hand
Remember the times you threatened to end my life
Remember the times you threatened to take my daughter an send her to your country,
Remember the times you tell me I will not see my daughter any more
You remember the times you tell me you would make my daughter have no respect for me,
You remember the times you took all my money
You remember the times I had to ask you for money
You remember the many times you ask me what I need money for
You remember you choose my clothing for me when we went shopping
And if I did not like what you choose you would take my hand bag and live me with no money to get home do you remember now
You remember the time you cut up all my important documents so I will not live you
You remember sure you remember stop pretending
Stop telling people you never did those things to me
I did not make those things up
They really happen
And it happen to me
And you did it

I am no longer live in your home any more
Stop making people think that I am crazy
You made me think that I was crazy when I was living with you
No more, no more
I am not crazy
And I am not stupid
Your behaviours has affected our daughter

I AM

I am tired of being haunted by your Beatings
I am tired of being tormented by your swearing and yelling's
I am tired of being a slave to Fear
I am tired of shedding tears

I am tired of feeling Sadness
I am tired of feeling depress
I am tired of sleepless nights
I am tired of feeling guilty

I am tired of feeling stupid
I am tired of feeling this small
I am tired of lying
I am tired of covering up for you

I am tired of the blame game
I am tired of the beatings
I am tired of the yelling
I am I tired of the swearing

I am tired of being manipulated
I am tired of being accused
I am tired of wasting my time and energy on you
I am tired, I am tired

I am tired of feeling ashamed
I am tired of Loss of appetite
I am tired of the weight gain
I am tired of not talking to my friends

I am tired of cannot go anyway
I am tired of cannot choose for myself
I am tired of cannot do things for myself
I am tired of being abused

I am just tired

NO MORE

No more pain
No more sadness
No more depression
No more lies
No more loneliness
No more tears
No more manipulations
No more beatings
No more yelling
No more swearing
No more if you love me
No more I love you that why
No more mind games
No more guilty feelings
No more confusion
No more craziness
No more feeling stupid
No more fear
No more feeling degrading
No more put downs
No more torment
No more feeling crazy
No more feeling small
No more feeling degraded me in the present of my daughters
No more feel fear to go to bed at night
No more fear to speak for myself any more
No more mess in my life
No more negativity
No more toxic relationship
No more dis-believe
No more destructive behaviour
No more disappointments
No more feeling helpless
No more blaming
No more complaining
No more dishonesty
No more wondering
No more argument

YOU CALL ME DEGRADING NAMES

You expect me to make love to you
You have no respect for me
How can I give my body to you?
What do you think of me?
You call me a stupid bitch
I maybe a bitch
But I am not your bitch

I don't want your filthy hands touching on me any more
I will never let you touch me any more
This body belongs to me
You act like if I am a piece of property
Well I am not
This body is the only one
I have and I have to take care of it

The look you give to me when you are mad or upset
The look in your eyes
The look on your face
The language you speak to me

The tone in you voice
The vain on your face and neck pop out
You swelled up like a porcupine

You refused to listen to me
You refused to take advice from me
You tell me you would never take advice from any woman
You asked me why you should take advice from me
Dam piece of shit woman like you
Stupid bitch like me

I AM PROUD TO MEET YOU ALL

I thank the lord for you all
Because you give so much
I am very thankful to you all
Thank you all for your love and support
This Is My Life

This is my life and I am taking controlled of my life
I am taking the power back from you
I have the power to controlled my own life
I have the power to controlled my destiny

I have the power to take controlled of my well-being
No one can take controlled over my life but me
I am the one person who holds the key to my life
I am the one in controlled
Not you no more

Did you really think that I cannot do anything without you; you are so very wrong? I don't need you to always tell me what I should do, I don't need you to always choose my clothing my shoes or tell me how I should style my hair, how I should put my make up on, you took it upon yourself to do those things because you said that I was stupid, I was not stupid I was scared of you so badly, and also to keep peace in the home I did what you wanted me to do because when you did not get your way you would make life un- bearable for our daughter and for myself in the home you would destroyed my things, you would break my things, you would cut up my clothing, you would yelled at me, swear at me, shout out degrading things to me, call me degrading names, there was no need for those things I am capable of doing things for myself and by myself, look at me now I am fine since I left you I am doing quite well I went back to school I am now working and I am taking very good care of my daughter and myself I don't need you now do I don't need you to hold my hands I have never need you to hold my hands you took it upon yourself it was not because you love me as you claim but because of your controlling behavior , today I am a much stronger, happier, confident person, I am not scared to express my thought's or say what's on my mind I am me again, I am myself again, I am the person you try so hard to breakdown and destroyed over the past eight years I am still standing stronger and standing stronger than before what you did to me was not love, you call that love I have news for you that was hate, hate with a passion

I dedicate this book to all shelter workers and social workers in Montréal, Québec and Calgary, Alberta and to all woman, men, children and families who has been affected by domestic abuse. Also, I dedicate this book to my daughter who gave me strength and the courage to carry on, and to my co-workers I could not write this book without any of you I hope that book would be an inspiration and encouragement to anyone who read this book. Thank you.

Life throws us curve balls sometimes we get knocked down, it is not staying down that matters but is how fast we get back up.

CPSIA information can be obtained at www.ICGtesting.com
Printed in the USA
LVOW130846280313

326376LV00001B/21/P